As Clean a Lot of Children as He Had Ever Seen

Edited by
Jane Seabrook

CTR Publishing
9 High Street
East Hoathly
East Sussex

1997

First published 1997

ISBN 0-9524516-1-1

Also published by CTR Publishing:
The Diary of Thomas Turner
Edited by David Vaisey

Printed and typeset by The Authors' Publishing Guild,
Maynards Green, Sussex TN21 0DG
Tel 01825 830319

INTRODUCTION

I should like to thank Mrs. Jackie Morris for originally allowing me to transcribe the School Log Books and also for agreeing in principle that a book should be published. I also thank Mrs. Paula Duff and the current School Governors for giving the final go ahead, and Mark Carter, Daniel Grima, Dexter Grima, Sarah-Jane Leyland, Ben Martin and Debbie Pellett for their excellent drawings.

My thanks also to all those people who have contributed post cards or photographs, and who have searched their memories to put names to the faces depicted therein; also for answering my many questions.

My thanks also to Les Hall for giving his time in designing the cover.

At the request of the Governors, certain names have been omitted because of the reason for the entry. However, should any reader be researching his or her family history, it is possible for these names to be given, plus any further entries which have had to be omitted for reasons of space.

There was a school at East Hoathly during the life time of Thomas Turner, the Diarist who lived in the village in the 1700's. He kept school for a year from April 1775, taking over from Thomas Tomsett who had died. He records that he negotiated the "hire of Mr. Virgoe's house to teach school in". He subsequently handed over to Francis Elless in 1776. The building now called The King's Head was referred to as "all that new-erected messuage or tenement and garden …commonly called the Schoolhouse".

It is clear from the Log Books started in 1865 at the opening of the newly built school that there were several Dame Schools in the area, all of which receive scathing comments from the East Hoathly headmasters.

There is much research to be done on this area of East Hoathly's history.

A percentage of the profits of the sale of this book are for School Funds.

East Hoathly Schools

IN THE BEGINNING

Captain Clements whose name is in nearly every entry until his untimely death in 1900, was the chief instigator in the building of the schools. Captain Clements came to live in the village at Belmont in April 1861 and was soon enquiring into the schooling of the children. He was dismayed to find there was one room about ten feet square for the girls and a smaller one for the boys and the school accounts had a deficit of £50 or more.

He brought up the subject whilst dining with the Squire, Mr. Gilliat, and was promised £100 if he, Captain Clements, would raise the necessary funds. He was obviously a man of action as within two years the land had been acquired from the Church, the necessary money had been raised, the schools designed, built and opened. The local firm of Halls were the builders and the architect was Mr. Ewan Christian of Whitehall Place, London. The total cost of the school plus the master's residence was £861. On Thursday 19th January 1865 the Schools were dedicated and on Monday, 30th January opened for school work. At the time of building it was generally felt in the village that the project had got out of hand and there would not be enough children to fill the space, but in less than five years it became necessary for some additions to be built as will be seen from the extracts which follow.

Captain Clements died in 1900 as the result of an accident at Buxton where he was on holiday, and the entry recording his death is particularly poignant as it is edged round in black, an honour not given to any other, not even to Queen Victoria.

The then Rector, the Reverend Langdale, his wife and their daughters, and later the Reverend Harbord and his wife took a great interest in the day to day working of the school and were frequent visitors. The Langdale daughters also took lessons. The Squire lent his garden for the annual school treat, until his death when the Rectory garden was used instead.

The first Master was a Mr. W. B. Kingswood, and my first impressions of him were that he was from a town, as his entries betray an impatience for "this agricultural village". However, the census for 1871 reveals that he was born in Buxted. His entries are heavily underlined and he is obsessed with the attendance numbers. This is understandable when it is realised the success of the school, the grant and his salary are all linked to the number of children and their regular attendance. The Government grant for the first year was £30 3s. 9d. and in 1899 when the numbers of children had risen the grant was £137. There is annoyance that the children are used by the parents to "tend baby" whilst they work in the fields and that the children are also employed. But, of course, money was short, some children being unable to return to school after the hop-picking holidays as they could not be "rigged out" because their parents had not been paid for the work done.

Mr. Kingswood stayed with the school for six years, leaving in August 1871 and then begins the long association between the village and the Jones family, for the father, Frederick Jones was followed by his two sons who became Masters after him, Mr.

Capt. Henry Topham Clements

Frederick Thomas Jones unfortunately dying after five years in office, when his younger brother Ernest Alexander took his place.

The Victorian Schoolmaster was a stickler for obedience, good behaviour to others and cleanliness and this is confirmed by many entries. We have no exact record of discipline, but there are a few entries which occur in the Log Books, and these would be unacceptable to-day!

The "gentry" visited the schools often, particularly in the beginning, bringing visitors with them to see the children at their work and most particularly to hear them sing and perform their drill. The children were the recipients of a great many treats provided by the gentry; they gave parties to celebrate the marriage of their sons or daughters, and any national event such as a Royal Wedding; they donated prizes for the annual school examinations; they provided Christmas treats and also paid for the annual outing which surprisingly was on many occasions to the Crystal Palace. The children were given sweets, oranges, apples, toys and games.

The school was in every way the pride of the village and of the Master and Managers. It was regularly inspected, cleaned and painted inside and out. The little annoyances, particularly with the children's "offices" are also chronicled. New equipment is mentioned so we have an insight into how the children were taught. It was also closely linked with the Church, hence the great emphasis on Scripture and all the examinations and Prize giving.

The school buildings also appear to double as the village hall, many entries noting that the school was closed early as the room was needed for an entertainment of some kind or other.

The weather plays a very large part in the smooth running of the school, as many of the children had two or more miles to walk each way, each day. One year appears to be exceptionally wet, particularly at the time the children are on their way, so they all arrive extremely wet and cold, and are sent home again, the school being closed. The weather in Victorian times would seem to have been far more extreme than now - there were frequently severe snowstorms with deep drifts and the roads impassable. Roads were merely successive layers of broken stone or flint and in the 1890's this would have been rolled by steam roller in order to make a smoother surface.

Illness ran through the school like wildfire and some were diseases which are heard of but little these days. There were epidemics of smallpox, diphtheria, ringworm, scarlet fever, impetigo, influenza and, of course, mumps, chickenpox and measles. And everyone suffered from continual colds and coughs - and chilblains.

It is very easy to jump to the wrong conclusion when reading records of this kind, but I have tried to verify my facts, and should I have misconstrued anything and in so doing offend anyone, then please accept my assurances that this was not what was intended. In making this transcription, I have left the punctuation (and some spelling) as written and it will be noted that Mr. Kingswood in particular is very fond of capital letters in some surprising places! and each head master had his own way of abbreviating the more commonly used words.

View of East Hoathly Church

1865

*W. B. Kingswood, Schoolmaster. S. A. Kingswood, Sempstress.

The School was formally opened on January 19th 1865.

Service was performed in the Church at 2 p.m. after which the Parents and Children were regaled with Cake and Tea in the New Schoolroom. Before partaking of this repast, the Revd. Edward Langdale, Rector of the Parish read a few prayers - a Form prepared for the occasion thus duly opening the Schools. Edwd. Langdale Rector.

* Certificated, 3rd Class, 1st year

Jan. 30   The School was to-day opened for schoolwork, the Revd. E. Langdale reading Prayers. The weather was most unfavourable, yet the numbers in the morning were 34 and in the afternoon 35. Found several children of 12 years of age and upward, but certainly all bear sad traces of neglected education and bad management. The majority were boys admitted to-day - several of whom are the sons of Master Tradesmen and Farmers, who shew unmistakable signs of having been taught under the old Commercial School regimen. Some, when interrogated, having advanced as far as "Barter", and when asked to put down the simplest number, containing a cipher, failed to do so; evidently all <u>rote learning</u>. No <u>Reason</u> for anything. No <u>Revision</u> of anything. The Writing very poor scrawl. The Reading, <u>hurried</u> and no <u>expression</u>.

Feb. 2   Arranged the School into four Standards according to the requirements of the R[evised] Code. Revd. Langdale and Party visited us in the afternoon.

Feb. 6   Admitted 36 New Scholars to-day. Engaged the whole morning in arranging into Standards. Miss E. Langdale kindly assisted in the morning by taking one of the lower Standards. Mr. R. B. Jones took Standard 1 in Reading and arithmetic

Feb. 8   Ordinary progress. Was arranging standards at intervals during the day. Miss E. Langdale took her usual Class in the morning and so did Mr. Jones. Revd. E. Langdale, Capt. and Mrs. Sargeant visited Schools in afternoon. The Master's New Desk and the Governess' New Table both arrived to-day. They are really useful Articles in a School.

Feb. 13   Snowy. Several absent in consequence. Mr. R. B. Jones acted as an assistant to-day. The Revd. E. Langdale and Miss E. Langdale, with Mrs. Clements, visited school in the afternoon. Kept a Boy in half an hour for laughing during prayers.

Feb. 17   …The Average this week is reduced, from the falling off of little ones, on account of the Wet Weather. The Average 69.

Feb. 21   Good attendance to-day and fair amount of Work done.

Revd. E. Langdale visited in the afternoon and reported of the bad behaviour of certain Boys, who were duly cautioned by me as to their future conduct in going from School and at other times.

Mar. 1   Better attendance to-day; All the Elder children (about 50) attended service at Church at 11 o'clock, being Ash Wednesday. The New Easel and Blackboard, 2 Stands and additional Books arrived to-day.

Mar. 6   Many absent through Wet. Had to very severely talk to several boys, on account of very improper conduct. The two ring-leaders were kept in at night and well admonished. Sorry to find among several of the boys, a great liking for immoral conversation and actions, but impute it to their associating with many low companions, who have scarcely if any check upon them. Hope to instil a liking for better things in their minds, in course of time by punishing and admonitions.

Mar. 7   Better attendance. 82 in afternoon. Mrs. Clements and Mrs. F. C. Clements visited in afternoon and waited Prayers and saw Children dismissed. Had to give the children a severe lecturing about their idle and negligent conduct. Also reported same to the Visitors who expressed hopes of improvement among them.

Mar. 8   …Rather better attention by bigger Boys.

Mar. 10   …Standard IV entered Bill's of Parcels in Copy Books. Revd. E. Langdale took Standard II for 1 hour in morning. Mr. R. B. Jones has assisted during the week as usual. The Average 80 is as last week; it would have been higher but for the weather. Monday having been a very wet day. Planted 3 Ivy plants around the School which were given by Miss Langdale.

Mar. 16   …Revd. E. Langdale, Captain Clements and Company visited in the morning and planted the trees in corners of the School Grounds.

Mar. 20   North East wind dreadfully cold and many away SICK in consequence…Also visited by Dr. Holman, Captain Clements, Mrs. Clements, Mrs. and Miss Langdale and the Revd. Lea and Mrs. Lea of Waldron. Could not do much in School on account of the Children continually coughing and the Chimnies smoking.

Mar. 23   Standard IV wrote a letter in Copy Books to-day. Took all in singing to Harmonium morning and Evening…

Mar. 27   …Admitted two children. Several away through sickness…The New Cupboard in use for first Day.

Apr. 3   Many sick ones back to-day. Admitted four new scholars. Captain Clements and friends visited in afternoon and ordered additional blind to Class Room…

Apr. 5   Good School to-day…Caroline Elphick began to-day as Stipendary Monitor.

Apr. 7   Ordinary progress. Sickness better this week. Many returned. Average for week 90. Admitted Four. Out of 111 on our books we had during week 102 present.

Apr. 10   Good school. Very hot. Children very lazy. Both rooms full…

Apr. 11 …The whole of the Committee held a meeting in School at noon, when a New Eight Day Clock was presented to the school by Wm. Gilliatt, Esqr. Miss Langdale visited school in the afternoon and took singing class. Governess being unwell the Girls were obliged to leave work at 3 p.m. and come into their classes.

Apr. 17 Good school considering its being Easter Monday …Admitted Four new scholars and was obliged to give orders that the little boy H. T. should not come any longer as he was so dreadfully tiresome.

Apr. 18 …By Order of Committee sent Lucy Funnell home as Small Pox prevails near her house and she mixes with the children.

Apr. 19 Several away to-day from divers causes. One family of 5 on account of a report that "The Bad Throat" prevailed among some of the scholars

Apr. 25 …Several away "minding baby" while mother's hoptying.

Apr. 26 …Heat quite overcoming in the Afternoon.

May 1 Good school. Took Children for a walk through the Village in the afternoon and had a nice game in the Field. Before parting they were all regaled with food and Drink given by Members of the Committee. Several pieces were sung by the Children during afternoon. Believe that such an afternoon's recreation produced good effect among the children and is calculated to excite good impressions of the School among the Parents.

May 3 Took Standards 3 and 4 in morn. in a lesson of Geography from Sullivan's Geo: Generalized. Found them very ignorant of the first principles of Geo: and were very pleased with the lesson.

May 9 Kept 2 boys in till 5 p.m. for coming late, and several others for idleness in afternoon's work…

May 18 Several absent to-day - their Mothers hoptying. Discovered a girl stealing another's dinner, whom I admonished and Kept in…

May 31 Caught a Girl, named L. T. thieving a second time. Made her stand on Bench with ticket marked "Thief" on her back. Laughton Club and several there whose parents are Members…

The Clubs which appear with great regularity in the records, particularly the Village Club and The Bat and Ball Club, were clubs started as benefit societies. A subscription was paid and in theory when the subscriber became ill he could call upon the Club for benefit. Unfortunately, sometimes the funds would all be squandered on a Club Day with festivities and jollity for everyone. However, as the Village Club, Laughton Club, the Bat and Ball Club, and others mentioned here continue throughout the years, one can assume that they were correctly conducted to the benefit of the subscribers. The East Hoathly Benefit Society published their balance sheet in May every year. In 1880 they had a feast and held "athletic and rural sports". But in 1883 it was reported that a dinner ticket and 1s. only would be distributed on feast days which was felt to be a "step in the right direction" although it was considered by some that it would have been preferable to keep all the funds for sick distribution.

June 12   Considering it the first day after the Whitsun Vacation, and that Haying has commenced in the Parish, we had a tolerably good school…

June 19   …Cautioned boys against teasing the cattle in Mr. Rich's Field.

June 21   …Kept a batch in after school for being late.

July 5   …Fred Leeson one of the Standard I Boys, who died on Friday was interred to-day, close by the School Yards. Several of Standard IV were away in afternoon playing a match against the Waldron Lads.

July 6   …Heat very great. The Children quite prostrated.

July 10   Fair attendance. Few away as it was wet early in the morning. Had occasion to send two children home on account of its being reported that a certain disease prevailed in their House. Intend to ascertain the accuracy of the report.

July 21   Ordinary progress. The Second Quarter of this School expires to-day. The School has Kept up well. Illness has prevailed somewhat largely and in 1 case has proved Fatal. Haying took very few away and those Chiefly among the little ones to mind the Baby. There has been a Fair number of Visitors who have expressed themselves generally pleased with the routine of the School and the demeanour of the Scholars. The Average attendance for Quarter is 88 being ten in excess of last. The admissions, which have been one or more almost every week, have been chiefly among the Infants.

There were no official holidays at all, but the school year was divided into quarters and there was a definite date to the end of the old year and the beginning of the new one. In 1869 this occurred at the end of March. This was the time when the Head Master submitted his report on the school year to the Managers. Details of the school's progress and finances were published in the local paper each year. The length of the summer holidays was always governed by the state of the hop harvest.

However in 1927 J. H. Baines, Director of Education wrote regarding the holidays - all public elementary schools should be open on at least 420 half days during the year, thus allowing a maximum of 100 half days for holidays. Then the holidays were listed as follows:- Christmas holiday was to be 18 - 24 half days depending where Christmas day fell. Easter and Whitsun were firmly fixed and the summer holiday was up to the Managers, and a margin of 14 - 20 half days to be used at the discretion of the Managers. The Christmas, Easter and Whitsun holidays had to be adhered to, except some variations were allowed for the Christmas and Whitsun holidays in those schools affected by hoppicking.

July 24   Children troublesome, the heat so oppressive…

July 31   School rather less to-day. Harvest has begun and several away. Revd. E. Langdale and Captain Clements visited in morning and brought intelligence of the time - May 66 - when we might expect Her M. Inspector.

The Inspector's visit took place once a year, the older children leaving immediately afterwards to take up their employment and the rest of the pupils moving up to their new Standards, and children fresh from the Infants would form Standard I (7 year olds). There was no Standard VII (13 year olds) until 1882. Pupils were admitted, and re-admitted throughout the year as necessary.

It was an important point in the school year, in that all children were examined individually to assess the efficiency of the teaching, and to fix the amount of the Head Teacher's salary, and the amount of the Grant the authorities would pay. The Head Teacher's salary was based on the children each making a sufficient number of attendances in the school year. In 1833 Parliament had put aside about £20,000 which was to be distributed to local managers for organising schools.

Under the Revised Code for Elementary Education introduced in 1862 the Government would pay 12s. for any child on the school's register; of this 12s. one third was paid for those pupils making a certain minimum number of attendances in a school year, the minimum being 200. If a child did not make this minimum, then the 4s. was lost. In addition, the Government paid 8s. for every child who passed the Inspector's examination in reading, writing and arithmetic, i.e. 2s. 8d. for each subject. This system would, of course, not take into account any child who had what we today would call "special needs". This was the total amount of money coming in, plus the fees paid by the children themselves. This amounted to 2d. a child for one child and 3d. for two children from the same family. From these small amounts the Managers had to pay salaries, maintain the buildings and heat them. It was therefore very important to see that the children attended school, learned their lessons and attended school on examination day. There are several references in the Log Books to the Master "rounding up" children for the day in question.

Aug. 14   Fair School to-day considering the advanced state of Harvesting. Visited in afternoon by Mrs. and Miss E. Langdale and Lady Friends who witnessed dismissal and expressed approval with state of the School. Mercy Fears who was here as late as Wednesday last was taken ill of Bronchitis and died on Sunday morning. Thus making the second who has died suddenly among the lower Standard in the course of a few weeks.

Aug. 18   Broke up today for Hoppicking…

Oct. 2   School commenced to-day after the Harvest and Hoppicking Holidays. Numbers good being over 100 both morning and afternoon. Revd. Ed. Langdale visited in the morning. Some old Scholars re-admitted and some fresh ones entered.

Oct. 4   …School Treat in afternoon.

Oct. 19   The children had a Holiday to-day of a grand Treat at the Residence of one of the Managers, W. Gilliat, Esqr. on the occasion of the marriage of Miss Gilliat.

Oct. 24   …The whole School left at 3 p.m. to go to the Grounds of Captain Clements to pick up Chestnuts, he having kindly given permission.

Nov. 14   Re-admitted a Boy, John Fears who has been away all summer. Obliged to stop work at 3.30 being dark and wet.

Dec. 1   The weather, having been finer this week, there has been better attendance. The Revd. Ed. Langdale very kindly interceded for the bigger Boys and obtained a fine Foot-ball and gave them a lesson in the game in their dinner-hour. Average this week 105.

Dec. 5   Revd. Langdale visited and complained of the Boys cutting sticks in his grounds. He cautioned them against doing so in future. A Mrs. E. who sends her child about the most irregular in the whole school accuses the Stipendary Monitor of harsh treatment - viz. "holding hands over head" - and makes that the excuse for Keeping her at home for the past 3 weeks. I find the girl had to hold her hands up with two others for play and say that the teacher was justified in so doing. Through the irregular attendance, the child is a perfect dunce and can do nothing but "play". A few of this sort in the school are more trouble and anxiety than the whole lot put together…

Dec. 19   Before dismissal this afternoon the Testimonial subscribed for by the Teachers and Children was presented to Miss E. F. Langdale on her leaving for India in token of the deep sense of gratitude and esteem felt by all. Examination for Prizes was continued through the day.

Dec. 21   Broke up to-day for "Xmas-week". Distribution of Prizes took place in the morning by W. Gilliat Esqr., who was attended by Revd. E. Langdale and Family. Mrs. and Miss S. Gilliat, Captain and Mrs. Clements, Mr. and Mrs. H. Holman, Mr. Thos. Holman, etc.

1866

Jan. 22   Wet yet a good school. Over 100 present. Admitted 1 Girl. Miss C. Langdale took Infants an hour in the morning. G. T. broke the first pane of Glass (since the school has been opened) in the Lobby.

Jan. 29   Many away sick to-day and could scarcely work for the noise caused by the coughing of those here…

Jan. 30   Ordinary progress. Cautioned the Children against the growing evil of asking to leave school before the proper [time], unless in very urgent cases. Refused to allow two families to go.

Feb. 19   Kept a lot of "late comers" in to-day as a caution to themselves and others.

Feb. 20   None late this afternoon. The simple punishment being enough. Mrs. Langdale took the sewing class with the Governess in the afternoon. A Boy, Geo. Evenden, was almost on the point of falling in another fit, but I caught him in time and after sitting by the fire a short time, seemed quite recovered. The cold seems to affect him.

Feb. 26   Children report to-day of losing things out of their dinner baskets. Cautioned the school against such practices.

Feb. 27   Mrs. Langdale assisted in needlework this afternoon. Scolded some of the children for come[ing] dirty and untidy.

Mar. 5   Several away to-day from unknown causes…Miss C. Langdale took Infants a short time in the morning. Cautioned the children about throwing and stopping the watercourses in the neighbourhood.

Mar. 13   Took Standard IV in Extra Lesson in Proportion instead of Reading. From Complaints by Revd. Ed. Langdale I reprimanded the children for making gaps in hedges etc.

Mar. 21   Weather very cold, a few away in the afternoon on account of wet. Kept 7 children in for various petty offences. Obliged to take more than the usual numbers of monitors to assist the lessons requiring their assistance.

Apr. 9   First day after the Easter Vacation. Cold and Wet. Many away being Easthothly Fair.

The Easthothly Fair was an annual event and always caused many of the children to be absent, as did the Ringmer Steeple Chase and other such happenings in the district. The Easthothly Fair seems to have had rather a chequered history in the late Victorian times, some years the trade was dull with no quality animals and other times trade was brisk. In 1887 the sheep were in short supply, only 300 being sent; one can only speculate on the numbers that constituted a good supply! There was also "300 head of cattle, business very dull". The day always concluded with dinner at the King's Head.

Apr. 11   Very wet in afternoon. Many away. Kept A. E. and A. W. till 5 o'clock for wickedness and I. R. for using bad language.

Apr. 18   …Edward Paris accidentally cracked a pane of glass in the Lobby.

May 1   The children were regaled with cake and tea etc. in the afternoon when many of the gentry were present. The Treat - to commemorate the marriage of Miss Emma Langdale on Feb. 11/66 in Calcutta. The Treat was entirely given by the Revd. E. Langdale and 130 Day and Sunday Scholars were the grateful recipients.

May 7   Usual work. A Great many children with colds and coughs, almost at times unable to proceed from the noise of the coughing.

May 14   Admitted three new scholars. Many away from various causes. Sickness the principal one but some from Hoptying, Kick-pulling and Taw-flowing.

May 31   Several away to-day from various causes. In the afternoon to attend a Tea party in the Village.

June 7   Several away to-day. Could not be got ready this morning and some sick from having eaten so much Trash at the Club yesterday.

June 11   Admitted three fresh scholars to-day. Had occasion to punish some children for trespassing in Mr. Rich's premises.

June 12   Usual progress. The Afternoon work was as the morning for the girls had but little sewing so the Governess assisted in the teaching.

June 21   The Children were treated to-day in the afternoon by H. Holman Esq. being the Wedding of Miss H. Holman, a Sunday Teacher.

From the East Sussex News:- "The children of the National School to the number of 140 with suitable banners marched in procession, headed by the excellent schoolmaster and mistress and were entertained on the grounds at Gate House, and afterwards were regaled with tea and plum cake in the School room." Mr. Holman was one of the surgeons in the village.

July 18   Kept several loiterers in till six in the Eve.

July 23   "Bat and Ball Fair". Several away from the Whitesmith District.

Aug. 10   Excursion to the Crystal Palace. Day's Holiday granted by the Managers. ...

There are few details of the excursion, but the East Sussex News reports that "many of our parishioners who accompanied by most of the school children had a holiday…They were by the kindness of the Earl of Chichester and William Gilliatt, Esq. conveyed to Uckfield early in the morning, and from thence took train and were soon whirled to the Palace where they were much gratified by the sights and wonders therein…" The railway had come to Uckfield in 1858 and by 1863 excursion trains were transporting the population all over the country.

Aug. 20   …Hooping Cough has just made its appearance, helping to thin our ranks still more…

Aug. 24   Broke up to-day for the usual Hoppicking Holidays of one month. The school has gradually fallen off this week, the Harvesting being in full operation. We break up a week later than last year.

Sept. 24   Resumed our school work to-day with only 20 children, as Hoppicking is not over and many children have the whooping cough. It is also very wet and dirty …

Oct. 9   …The Girls taken by the Teacher of Sewing in the large Room. I find it answers better than having the Infants in the same room with the Elder Children.

Oct. 31   Revd. E. Langdale taught a Standard this morning. The whole school went on the Grounds of Captain Clements Chestnutting at 3 in the Afternoon by his kind permission.

Nov. 7   …Revd. E. Langdale visited in the morning, to whom the bad behaviour of two Boys in Standard V was reported. He very kindly admonished them as to their future conduct.

Nov. 12   …First Fires to-day.

Nov. 19   Many away to-day. Admitted a boy from Ripe parish, aged 11 years, a very bad scholar, who has been only to a Woman's school on the Dicker and sadly neglected. We have also to enter another death - Clara Barnard - of the Nursery after a short illness.

Nov. 20   …Had to speak to the children before dismissal in the afternoon on their thoughtlessness in "talking" in school, the greatest "nuisance" with which a schoolmaster has to contend.

Nov. 28   Several absent in the afternoon from various petty causes. Lord Chichester visited in the afternoon and expressed his regret at seeing "Damp Walls" and not battened. He, else, likes the schools and Houses and the general appearance of the children.

Nov. 29   Ordinary progress, under difficulties, one or two (one as leader) of the Standard V Boys, behaving very badly after repeated cautions and beseechings.

Dec. 20   Broke up to-day for the Xmas holiday. The Managers and Ladies attended in the afternoon to distribute the Prizes. The children were regaled with Buns, Nuts and Oranges in profusion and after singing a few of their pieces were dismissed.

Dec. 31   First day after the Xmas vacation and as usual numbers slack there being only between 70 and 80 present. There are several away through sickness.

1867

Jan. 16   Cold so great that scarcely any children could come.

Jan. 18   …Children with such Coughs and Colds could scarcely work what few there were of them. This week has been the worst week for attendance and weather since the opening of the School.

Jan. 21   The weather being finer over head and the roads trodden, there was rather a better muster to-day (about 40). Many are troubled with bad coughs, which causes great disturbance to the lessons.

Jan. 23   …Fearfully dirty and wet causing many to be absent.

Jan. 29   …Kept a boy in for throwing stones.

Jan. 30   Better school to-day. Had to keep another boy in for throwing and others for talking and various petty offences.

Feb. 1   The average this week has risen to 70, as the weather has been much more favourable. Several children are sick and prevented coming by bad Chilblains.

Feb. 27   More here to-day but could scarcely work on account of the coughing which prevails among them.

Mar. 6   Instead of the usual simultaneous Table lesson in the morning the upper Standards were viewing the Eclipse of the sun and having an explanation of it. Being "Ashwednesday" all except the Infants attended Church at 11 a.m. On account of the illness of the Seamstress the Girls worked with the classes in the afternoon, as they have had to do for some days.

Mar. 7   Very snowy and many absent. Revd. E. Langdale visited and took a Class in the morning, myself, being obliged, from "sore-throat" to keep quite quiet during the day.

Apr. 11   …Had to keep several boys in for being late a second time in the afternoon, through birds-nesting.

Apr. 17   A Girl who was absent yesterday gave this excuse for thus absenting herself "A man as I was coming along the road in the morning told me to go home as it looked like rain" This and many other equally as frivolous excuses are made as the reasons for the irregular attendance. The Parents do not try to keep them regular. The more the Master tries to urge on them the necessity of regularity the more do they think, in ignorance, that we are beholden to them for their attendance…

May 1   Being May-day the whole school spent part of the afternoon in outdoor amusements, as is done annually.

May 8   Had to punish A. W. with a stick and keeping in for continual Truant playing, having found all other means of no avail.

May 15   Visited in the morning by the Misses Borradaile and Friends and in the afternoon by a Gentleman from India.

June 4   …Received a note from D. B. to express his ignorance of the fact that <u>his two boys</u>, were particularly requested to be present at the Inspection. The Managers therefore will allow them to come again, but the boys for their careless indifference, are to be well talked to.

June 21   Ordinary progress. Haying and thin attendance. Had a note to Mr. B. of Laughton to say he might send his two Boys as before, because he acknowledges that 'twas not with his knowledge they were kept away on the day of the <u>Government Examination</u>.

July 23   .... "Bat and Ball" Fair caused the absence of several. What with the Fairs, Clubs, Wet days, Baby-tending etc. etc. 'tis a miracle that any real progress is made.

July 31   ....very full school....Kept a batch of talking children in to-day. The echo of the school-room even with the ordinary noise of daily routine is at times almost maddening, this alone, when my attention engaged another way seems to become a cover to those inclined to talk.

Aug. 14   Many away gleaning.

Aug. 16   Days holiday granted by the Managers to allow the Elder Children to visit the Crystal Palace with their friends.

Oct. 14   Better school to-day, 100 in attendance. Some absent in the afternoon, to look <u>on at a Sale in the Village</u> their Parents, I suppose, thinking six and seven week's holiday, just terminated, hardly enough for the dear children.

Oct. 15   ....Reminded the children of the necessity of using a little more soap and water previous to starting to school.

Oct. 16   ....Kept in a batch of "Inattentives", and again scolded many for coming so dirty and ragged.

Oct. 24   Several absent today picking up acorns.

Nov. 11   A good school to-day, but some absent from sickness and I find from enquiries made that the Measles has broken out among them, if so, I fear the school will suffer in numbers for some months.

Nov. 18   <u>Measles, Coughs and Colds</u> are doing their work very fast.   Have sent several home very poorly and most of the children are very unwell.

Nov. 19   Ordinary work under difficulties, as the children are continually coughing and 37 are reported sick, most of them with the measles.

Dec. 2   Only 34 in attendance to-day.   <u>Cold extremely severe</u>. Measles very bad and general.

Dec. 16   Admitted a new scholar to-day, a boy of 12 years, but has only been to infants and women's schools and consequently for his age knows next to nothing. Revd. E. Langdale visited in the morning and at his request I cautioned children not to injure the paths, etc. etc.

Dec. 18   ....Children in upper standard writing their Xmas Letter to their Parents to-day.

Dec. 24   We "broke up" to-day for the usual Xmas Holidays. The Children in the afternoon were visited by the Revd. and Mrs. Langdale and Family and the Misses Borradaile and Company, who very kindly distributed among those present Oranges, Nuts, etc. etc.

1868

Jan. 6   Resumed duties after Xmas Vacation. Weather very inclement but had 60 in attendance. Many of the Infants away on account of the weather. Infant Mistress has not returned, not being sufficiently recovered from previous illness…Admitted three new scholars, all of a long age, but residents out of the parish and thorough dunces, having attended dame schools principally or some little better. They ought to be fit for Standard Six, but really only suitable for Standard II.

Throughout the Log Books, each head teacher has nothing good to say for the "education" given by these dame schools; all children who attend East Hoathly school who have previously been elsewhere are labelled ignorant, knowing nothing and put into the lowest possible standard.

Jan. 18   Fine to-day. Several returned to-day who have not been since Xmas, and therefore rather behind their Standard, causing <u>more</u> work, and <u>more</u> noise, for as a general rule, I find the more irregular they attend, the less inclined to care to work are they when here…

Jan. 21   …To-day we have been furnished with another of the many illustrations of the little care felt for children by parents and Guardians, as respects their regular attendance. A little boy brought word, as a reply to whether his little brother was not coming now it was fine weather, that "She would send him when she thought she would." This message was sent by an elder sister who keeps her father's house, through her little brother who is in the Infant Department.

Jan. 31   A considerable number absent in the afternoon of to-day. I have often noticed the same thing and cannot conceive why they (especially the Infants) should thus be allowed to spend Friday Afternoon at home, unless their Parents, fear that Saturday and Sunday, will scarcely be sufficient time for them to hear their dear voices at home, and to wear out their clothes, etc.…

Feb. 4   More absentees, through sickness, several cases of Scarlet Fever in the district following on the heels of the Measles. A Committee meeting to-day at the Schools…Strictly cautioned children about destroying the fences of Mr. Benham and other little misdemeanors.

Feb. 11   …To-day, to help to stimulate in the children the love for reading I sold 12 dozen cheap Periodicals, back numbers, obtained cheap at the Book-sellers in Lewes. About 65 children became purchasers and cleared away the whole lot.

Feb. 25   …The Revd. E. Langdale admonished the children, at my request, respecting a rather common and lightly thought of failing, viz. using obscene and filthy language one to another. I am sorry to add, that I find those children most guilty of so doing, who, from Knowledge, I know have sad examples, not 100 miles from their own homes.

Mar. 24   …Several absent to-day <u>this</u> day of the week being the General Washing day.

Mar. 30   Not so full a school to-day, altho' fine. Mondays, I find, in this agricultural district is in several instances kept as "Saint

Monday". Several have gone to work a short time, "bird-tending" etc. etc.

Apr. 2   All the Bigger children attended the funeral of W. Gilliat, Esqr. this morning at 9.30, this gentleman being one of the Managers and liberal Supporters of these Schools.

Apr. 13   What with the sickness and it's being Easter Monday the school was thin to-day.

Apr. 27   Better school to-day. Some back who have been ill. Coughs very troublesome. Admitted three new scholars, two of whom aged respectively 8 and 9 years Knows nothing!!!

May 1   By permission of the Managers the afternoon of to-day was spent in amusements and procession as usual on May day.

May 18   …A hard job to keep the children up to the working mark as the heat was so excessive…The Infant Mistress being unwell, two Girls under my supervision managed them to-day.

June 10   …Punished two boys for trespassing on other land, and risking their necks by climbing fir trees.

June 29   …We issued to-day to the Subscribers and Parents of the Children our Annual Report and Balance Sheet.

July 2   One child, on being interrogated to-day as to the reason of his and his brothers' absence yesterday candidly and I believe truthfully asserted that he stopped at home "to play"!!!

July 7   Kept two boys in for taking other children's food from their basket.

Some of the pupils lived as far as two miles from school, so would have taken their lunch with them. Others went home, and sometimes did not return for the afternoon session, to the annoyance of the head teacher. From a timetable of 1880-1881 we can see the children had one and threequarter hours break from 12 o'clock, and in 1884 it had become 2 hours, in 1908 it was reduced to one and a half hours.

July 22   …Heat very oppressive, the Thermometer standing as high as 85 in the school.

Aug. 5   …Too hot to do much. The Children "Knocked-up".

Aug. 6   Wet to-day. Having been dry and fine so long about 30 were frightened to stay at home, so had only 32 here…

Sept. 24   Few absent in the afternoon as the Barham Hoppickers were being paid…

Sept. 28   Admitted and re-admitted several scholars to-day. There was also a better school, the children having been "rigged" out after hoppicking.

Oct. 13   …Several absent to-day picking up potatoes and acorns.

Oct. 23   …Admitted one new scholar, who has been to a Dame School at Ringmer and like almost all of those we get from adjoining parishes, knows little or nothing.

Nov. 4   A committee meeting held today and notes sent by their authority to parents whose families attend irregularly.

Nov. 10   121 attended in the morning and 122 attended in the afternoon of to-day, making one of the best days for attendance since the opening of these schools…

Dec. 1   The fullest school to-day ever known here viz. 129 present at once in the morning…

Dec. 14   …Very wet in afternoon and so dark that we had to dismiss by a quarter to four.

Dec. 18   Attendance to-day 121. Revd. E. Langdale, and Mrs. Langdale and Family with Mrs. Borradaile and Miss E. Borradaile visited in the afternoon and heard the school sing their Christmas Carols, etc. and looked at their Christmas letters. They then distributed oranges, Nuts etc. and the school "broke up" for a fortnights holiday.

1869

Jan 11   110 in attendance this morning but several absent, from colds etc. and fear several others will stay away from same cause, as a great many have coughed the whole day and seem quite poorly.

Jan. 26   …Kept a Batch of "bad behaved-ones" in after school.

Jan. 27   A boy named A. F. has played the Truant to-day and if I don't forget will be duly attended to tomorrow for his trouble. The act of "Truanting" is a very uncommon occurrence.

Jan. 28   …I tried to make some impression on the boy referred to yesterday as a "Truant".

Mar. 10   Two children, A. and E. H. were dismissed the school to-day because of the insulting behaviour of the mother, towards the Teacher for the third time. This was done at the instance of the Managers, after consultation.

Mar. 11   A calm has followed yesterday's storm. The atmosphere seems purer and with the exception of a faint and expiring gust or two all seems abated.

Mar. 16   I find several away "Rook-tending" one of them I understand only 6 years of age and belonging to the Infants.

Apr. 6   Admitted 1 new scholar to-day. The "Glass Pock" is very prevalent among the children and several are away ill with it…

Apr. 14   …More failed to-day with the "Glass-pock".

Apr. 16   The school shut to-day, by order of the Managers on account of sickness among the children. Chiefly in the Infant Department.

Apr. 29   …Several absent in the afternoon, supposed to be at Miss Bonnick's sale.

May 13   …One of the scholars broke her arm coming to school this morning by falling off a stile.

May 26   Revd. E. Langdale cautioned the school against the sin of swearing and particularly the family of M. who are very guilty of that wicked practice. Kept a batch of children in for getting into the wood and driving the cows during the dinner hour.

July 15   It required a great amount of patience and forbearance to-day, the heat of the crowded room producing such an amount of listlessness and idleness as is scarcely to be witnessed, except of a hot day in a country school.

July 19   By permission the Annual School Excursion to the "Crystal Palace" took place to-day.

July 22   …Several children (regardless of what I say against it) went home to dinner and did not return.

Aug. 26   Thursday. Broke up to-day for the usual months Hoppicking Holidays. There were 77 in attendance. Heat so great that children were quite unable to work. The schools were "broken up" rather earlier in order that the "Weather Tiling" might be commenced on the south side of the schools and School House.

Oct. 7   …Captain Clements visited in the morning and arranged for bracket to stand Globe on etc.

Oct. 22   …Mary Colman fell down coming to the school in the afternoon and broke the small bone of her arm.

Nov. 4   Sent a girl - M. A. G. - home for being impertinent to the governess. This is the kind of treatment we have to put up with, from children who are in a semi-barbarian state, through extremely irregular attendance or no instruction at all.

Nov. 11   …Had to punish a boy for being impertinent to Infant Mistress, when told by her of his faults.

Nov. 16   …Very full school, too full to do work anything like satisfactorily.

Nov. 25   …Upon making inquiry for a girl, S. E. , I was told by the monitor of her class to-day that her mother had kept her at home this afternoon, because he had put her name on the slate in the morning for some misdemeanour. The mother also signified her intention of going to the Revd. E. Langdale, as one of the Managers to acquaint him of the grievance - a very serious one, that we, the teachers should endeavour to keep as great amount of work going on, with as little talking and play as possible. Another girl, is also kept at home this week, because the mother of a girl who usually accompanies her to school and home, has ordered her girl not to go with her, because of her "rudeness" and bad conduct. This I believe to be quite correct as it is not the first time I have heard of her using indecent language etc. since being admitted to this school, from Newhaven where she appears to have laid up a very nice stock of filthy and disgusting ideas.

1870

Mar. 10   …Very full school. Mr. Hope, the Barber, cut 12 children's hair to-day.

Mar. 15   …School crowded too much to-day.

Mar. 16   A country school, as ours is, suffered in attendance to-day from Wet and inclement Weather…

Mar. 18   …Admitted two Infants this week raising our number on the books this quarter to 161.

Mar. 29   Several children afflicted with cold and coughs - the wind and weather being very inclement and severe. The mother of one of the children threatened to take her son from school, if he should by chance get into some squabble going home, about which the Master can have no knowledge or control. I cautioned the delinquent and admonished him not to retaliate again and I discovered as is the case in nine cases out of ten that "there was six of one and half-a-dozen of the other". The poor Schoolmaster generally comes in for his share of blame for every thing done in the parish by children. Parents can blame but 'tis rarely we are gratified by the humblest expression of gratitude for our efforts.

Apr. 11   …Since Friday last about 20 children have failed with "Mumps" and are still failing, having had to send several home to-day very poorly.

Apr. 25   Commenced duties after Easter Vacation. Many back who were sick. Several yet are ill and some even have failed to-day…

Apr. 26   …Captain Clements visited and left notices to be sent to all families (not belonging to the Parish) of extra-school fees to be paid on and after May 1st 1870.

May 2   The children had the Annual Mayday festivities this afternoon about 135 attended but several were kept at home, by sickness. Several keep failing with the mumps still. Many of the School managers and Ladies and several of the parents also attended. 32 Prizes were distributed consisting of Books, Writing Cases, and various useful articles as needlework prizes. The children were regaled with cake and Tea and spent a very happy afternoon.

May 13   The Diocesan Inspector examined the schools to-day. He came at 9.30 a.m. and stayed till 1.30 p.m. Expressed satisfaction at the state of the school and general intelligence of the Children.

Captain Clements and Revd. E. Langdale assisted in the examination. In a return furnished to Mr. Attenborough there were on the books 81 boys, 75 girls. Total 156.

From a book on Mayfield by Fred Lester, he describes the visit of the Diocesan Inspector: "…One of the great days arrived,…Mr. Westbrook [the head teacher] really was particular and on his toes all the time. We all had to come in our best clothes, faces washed, boots cleaned, hair brushed and all had to practice behaviour to meet the examiners…There we were all standing up alert, clear and attentive. Mr. Westbrook, the Rev. H. I. M. Kirby, Mr. Donald Barclay, [the two inspectors] a slight frail man, a magistrate with long white locks hanging down to his shoulders, a very stately figure…As the door opened, each bowed, Mr. Kirby bowed, Mr. Barclay gave a very stately bow…"

July 11   For four weeks, following the Whitsun Vacation, the school was closed, on account of the Scarlet Fever, which prevailed in the District. It re-opened to-day with 81 present. Many absent from various excuses and several reported as having left.

July 17   Excessively hot to-day, and 'twas with the greatest difficulty the children could be kept up to the mark.

July 18   The heat to-day with a crowded school was something fearful to stand. Several children were "Knocked up" with the heat.

July 26   A Few absent through the weather…The duties of the School were upset the last hour of the afternoon by a severe Thunderstorm which lasted sometime.

Aug. 8   Several of the Elder children who belong to the choir, were taken to Eastbourne to-day by the Misses Borradaile. Being very wet at noon several did not return from dinner.

Aug. 23   …About a week ago an adder was found in the passage coiled up under some clothes and to-day a large snake was killed by some of the Boys on the school premises, and in killing it a large frog, which it had gorged was crushed from it whole. Several back to-day which have been harvesting.

Sept. 2   Broke up for the usual Hop-picking Vacation, there were only 10 present the last day.

Sept. 26   The school re-opened to-day after three weeks vacation. Hoppicking not being finished there was a very thin attendance only 21 being present.

Oct. 3   About 50 in attendance to-day, the chief part of those absent being in the hop grounds. But they finish to-day…Admitted two new scholars, 8 and 6 years of age respectively, the girl at 8 being just able to spell 4 letters and can do nothing in counting on figures. The Boy knows only his Alphabet. They have been sadly neglected.

Oct. 4   Ninety in attendance to-day, this will be about the number this week, now. Several parents require a week, to new rig their children after hoppicking…

Nov. 23   In the afternoon there were several away, as the Clothing club was distributed.

Nov. 28   Several children who have now passed their sixth year were drafted in from the Infant Room into Standard one. But it causes the large Room to be much too full, there being over 80 in it this morning.

Nov. 30   Captain Clements and a Lady Friend visited and Sir James Duke with two other Gentlemen viewed the premises to-day.

1871

Jan. 9   …A great many are suffering, as well as myself, from broken chilblains.

Jan. 28   On Friday eve the 27th one of the Infants - Maria Fears - died from Diphtheria after a very short illness.

Feb. 6   Obliged to-day to report to the Revd. E. Langdale and Captain Clements two of the Managers who visited a case of insubordination. A boy, W. N., a second time in the space of a week, struck another scholar, when the Master's back was turned. Many yet away with colds and sore throats.

Feb. 21   …Revd. E. Langdale called and cautioned boys against throwing at the sound-hole in the Tower and throwing in general.

Mar. 1   The Foundation Stone of the New Infant School was laid to-day by Mrs. Borradaile. The Managers and other Ladies attended and all visited the schools before the Ceremony took place.

Mar. 6   Rather better attendance, but the coughing has been something dreadful. Bad colds seem spreading among the bigger children to-day. Had to send two home quite poorly…

Mar. 23　…The school week ended today as the bricklayers require to be in the room tomorrow, Friday, to remove the window…

The numbers of children attending school had been steadily rising until the largest number of 161 was reached in November 1870. In one entry Mr. Kingswood mentions that because some children from the Infants had come in to the Mixed School, those numbers totalled 80 children in one room. Of course, numbers were fluctuating daily, but it had become obvious that more room was needed.

Mar. 30　…the hammering etc. of the builders occasioned much noise. We willingly bear it knowing it "can't last"…

Mar. 31　…Had to reprimand several of the bigger boys for troublesome and unseemly behaviour at dismissal, it having become very general with them.

Apr. 11　…A great many absent especially in the afternoon. It is quite disheartening to try to keep them at school regularly. The parents appear so indifferent and keep them at home for every frivolous excuse.

Apr. 12　A wet morning, frightened a few, who, altho' it cleared early spent the whole day at home. Another way in which the parents shew their <u>anxiety</u> for the <u>childrens' progress</u>.

Apr. 28　Full school in the morning. In consequence of the great noise made by the workmen in finishing the new Room the children were dismissed at noon by the desire of several gentlemen of the Committee.

May 5　…On Wednesday the New Infants School was opened, the ceremony being attended by the Whole of the Managers and the Gentry of the District. Prizes were also distributed to deserving children.

May 12　The average this week has rather decreased. The treat being over…Dismissed R. L. as an incorrigible, having the consent of the Managers. Also "read the Riot Act" to several boys who spend their Evenings in the Street and annoy everybody passing and using filthy and abominable expressions within the hearing of some Ladies and Gentlemen and happening to be near I actually saw and heard the same. They were also insolent to Mr. and Mrs. and the Misses Benham…

May 26　…The hooping-cough has broken out in the school and several have failed this week and many more are "hatching" it.

June 9　…The Infants took possession of New School on Wednesday, the Classroom now being available for the Master, but the need of an <u>older and more staid</u> pupil teacher is much needed in order that the master may leave a class in his hands in the Class Room.

The post of pupil teacher had been created in 1846 to replace the monitorial system, and their conduct was strictly regulated. One pupil teacher was allowed for every 25 children, and the head teacher had to promise to give the pupil teacher the chance to observe and practise teaching in the school, and to personally instruct the pupil teacher for at least one and a half hours every morning or evening. When the five year apprenticeship (dating from leaving school at 13 years of age) had been satisfactorily completed, the pupil teachers would sit an examination for a Queen's Scholarship, with the aim of entering a training college for three years to become certificated teachers. There were many reasons why this level was not reached, but they could, at a lower salary, teach as uncertificated assistants.

In 1894 the Pupil Teachers went to Tunbridge Wells for their examination. It is noted that "their usual hour of instruction was changed from 7-8 until 12-1 so that for this week they could work at their drawings the examination taking place this day…The Pupil Teachers start work from 6.30-8 on Monday as is usual during the Summer months."

June 23   …I have proved that the Class Room, which now has been made available for the Master, since removal of Infants to new Room, can not be of much service, as the Stipendiary Monitor is too small and simple with the children, to be trusted out of my sight or to do anything effectual in it.

July 21   The Average Number of times attended by each child present at all this week is 3.9 as compared with 3.7 and 3.8 in the two previous weeks. This is owing to many children going home to dinner and staying to nurse while the mother goes "Haying". One girl has only been <u>one half day</u> and one boy only <u>one</u> day. The latter came to school on Tuesday morning dressed from top to toe in rags and filthy dirty, too. I sent him home at once and have not seen him since…

July 28   …Admitted a boy 9 years of age turned, but knows comparatively nothing, not fit for Standard I. These are scholars, which hurts schools in every way. He has been allowed to go to some private school, where, to <u>keep</u> the children and <u>get the pence</u>, the Mistress allows them to <u>do</u> as they <u>please</u> and <u>come</u> when they like. Exceptions to this are few.

Aug. 9 Captain Clements visited to-day and with the Managers consent, the school was closed till Monday Aug. 14th in order to enable me to pack my goods in readiness for removal on Friday 11th inst. A very good school and scarcely any sickness.

FREDERICK JONES
1871-1879

On the 14th August 1871 Mr. Frederick Jones, Certificated Master, 2nd Class, took charge, and so begins the very long association between the Jones family and East Hoathly School. As with all new Head Teachers he immediately set about examining the children to assess their capabilities.

Aug. 14   Frederick Jones having received the appointment as Master of these Schools commenced duties on Monday Morning. During the week all who have been present have undergone a searching examination. The Reading in the Upper Standards, Good. Third and Fourth, ditto, Fair. First Standard, Very moderate. The Reading very generally wants expression. The Writing is in many cases good, and in most fair. Spelling with the exception of the First Class very moderate, Arithmetic is very generally indifferent, and in the 1, 2, 3, 4, and 5 Standards very bad. Only an average of 3 sums in half an hour, and only one third of these correct. Geography in the first Class good. Mapping very fair. The cause of the Arithmetic being so indifferent seems to have been caused by the neglect of the Multiplication Table and Mental Arith…

Aug. 28   Received from Captain Clements a box of School materials chiefly for the infant school. The arithmetic in lower standards has this week received special attention…The Upper classes commenced Drawing this week…Weekly average 40.

Oct. 2   Mr. C. Borradaile visited the school on Monday morning and brought a packet of attendance cards. He also visited and inspected the writing on Tuesday morning…From the Register I find that E. A. will be presented in the 4th Standard next year, and yet she has been placed during the year with the Second standard and is still unable to do the Arithmetic and Spelling sufficiently advanced to pass in that Standard…

Oct. 30   …The Night School commenced on Tuesday evening. …The Arith: in the lower Standards has been very bad, The Multiplication Table is not known by some of the 5th standard, altered the Timetable to give more time to Tables.

Nov. 13   The Revd. Borradaile visited the School on Monday, and presented the boys with a new Foot-ball. At the same time he promised Two New Lamps for the Night School, which arrived on Thursday, and have proved of great utility…

Dec. 4   …Gastric fever rather prevalent. William Hancock, the Paid Monitor, has been ill. Captain Clements sent notices to the parents of M. A. G., L. W. , and M. H. requiring their attendance to be more regular, in default of complying with this requisition their names are to be struck off the Register.

1872

Jan. 8   …Mrs. Antram visited the School on Monday and distributed presents to those boys who were absent from the Xmas Treat. Miss Borradaile and the Revd. E. Langdale took a class on Friday Morning.

Mar. 11   …H. G., J. P. and G. T. punished for disobedience (repeat 30 lines of poetry)…

Apr. 29   On Wednesday the first of May the children paraded the village with garlands and banners and afterwards were treated with Tea, Cake etc. Rewards were distributed to the deserving children. Most of the resident gentry were present.

May 6   The average this week has decreased; the weather on several days being unusually severe. Many children have been taken away to assist their parents hop-tying …

July 1   The School was visited on Wednesday by Mr. George Borradaile and Miss Borradaile and after looking at the Writing, Mapping, Drawing he heard the First Class recite a portion of Henry the Eighth, the Pied Piper, and the Lay of the Last Minstrel. On Saturday those children who competed for prizes given by the Chailey Educational Union were examined by Captain Clements and the Revd. E. Langdale.

July 8   Captain Clements visited the School on Monday and brought two packets of new Attendance cards, these cards are specially framed to show the parents the Attendance and payments made by the children and are vastly superior to those previously in use…

July 15   New Rules and Cards issued to the children…The children who were examined on July 6th for the prizes given by the Chailey Educational Union, went on Saturday to Uckfield. The following were successful: E. Waldock first prize for Composition, History and Grammar. W. Noakes first prize for Geography and Dictation. Grace Jack first prize for Composition and Stocking Knitting, 2nd for Dictation. Sarah Parris first prize for Dictation, third for Composition. George Trill 3rd for Geography.

Aug. 12   Holiday. The Choir accompanied by a number of inhabitants of this village went to the Crystal Palace.

Oct. 7   Fair School. Commenced with Gardner and Sharps Home Lesson Books. Most of the parents consenting to purchase them, those who objected referred to Rule XI. The School supplies these Lesson Books at a great reduction.

Oct. 21   Night School commenced for the Winter. To be opened 60 Evenings (Three times a week for twenty weeks.) The Revd. Frederick Borradaile has kindly promised three prizes for best attendance.

Oct. 28   …On the occasion of the marriage of Mr. Thomas Holman each of the children were presented with a New Sixpence.

Nov. 18   Sent N. M. home again for breaking rule VIII. His parents have kept him at home for 5 weeks without permission. The Revd. E. Langdale brought him again the parents representing that the absence was caused through sickness. This excuse however cannot be entertained, for the boy was employed with his father the whole of the time.

1873

Jan. 27 …W. Noakes the first boy in the School left to go in a Warehouse in London.

Feb. 17 …On Monday gave the children an examination, with one or two exceptions they did very satisfactorily. Several of the Childrens times having become extremely precarious I visited the parents in order to urge them to send their children on every possible occasion.

May 1 The usual treat was given on the 1st of May by the Managers. The children gaily attired in floral decorations formed a procession and visited the residences of the gentry and after partaking of a bountiful repast in the School room, the successful children received handsome prizes. Writing desks, Books and Workboxes.

July 14 …The Revd. E. Langdale visited the School on Tuesday morning and reported that 9 children had obtained prizes from the Chailey Decanal Educational Union, viz.

To the best Scholar in the Union for
History: Eli Ashdown.
Neatness and Arrangement: Eli Ashdown.
Writing: Annie Sinden.
Spelling: John Burgess.
Mapping: George Trill.
Felling and Tucking: Agnes Luck.

To the Second Best Scholar in the Union for
Arithmetic: Eli Ashdown.
Dictation: George Trill.
Writing: Frederick Waldock.
Writing: Mary Russell.
History: Frederick Waldock.
Mapping Elizabeth Hancock.
Cutting out and making frock: Elizabeth Hancock.

To the Third Best Scholar for
Felling: Annie Sinden.
Writing: George Trill.
Cutting out and making Shirt: Mary Russell.
Dictation: Frederick Waldock.

Harry Hancock was awarded a prize for regular attendance.

To the Master was awarded a Certificate for the best School in respect of Writing, Arithmetic and also of Geography as equal with Chailey.

The Church Schools of the area were banded together in the Chailey Ruri-Decanal Educational Union and every year examinations and competitions were held for these schools. The prizes mentioned above are the first of many such. The Diocesan Inspector also called every year and examined the children in Scripture and the subsequent reports never vary with Excellent for practically all aspects.

July 28   At 12 o'clock on Monday morning Miss E. Borradaile commenced a Savings Bank for the benefit of the children.

Aug. 11   …Refused admission to an idiotic boy named A. from Chiddingly on the ground of age and non-residence in the Parish…

Oct. 13   …Several boys and girls employed at Barham, weeding…

Nov. 10   The two C.'s absent in the Afternoon. Kept at home because punished in the morning. As this was a rebellion against the discipline of the School the children being merely kept behind to do a greater quantity of Work, I gave notice that any future case should be brought before the School Managers when I should strongly press for a severe remedy.

Nov. 17   …The family of the W.'s Easthothly, were cautioned as to their excessively irregular attendance, the alleged reason being that they were employed gathering acorns.

Dec. 29   Commenced school after the Xmas Vacation with a fair School. On Friday morning the secular instructions began at nine in order that the School might be dismissed at Eleven, Mr. C. Borradaile having kindly consented to Exhibit a Magic Lantern to the children.

1874

Feb. 23   …On Friday the Night School was closed for the Winter. In consequence of the numbers excluded through being under and over age and two having passed all the Standards, the School will not be presented for examination this Winter.

Mar. 30   Fair attendance, several boys employed crowtending.

June 1   Commenced school after a weeks holiday…The G.'s and W.'s having determined not to pay the extra fees they were sent home until the rule was complied with.

June 22   On Saturday the First Class were assembled to undergo an examination in connection with the Chailey Educational Union, but after waiting 2 hours, it transpired that no "Questions" had arrived. This was a considerable disappointment to the children.

June 29   Ascertained that the papers were delayed by Post Office…

July 13   The successful children went to Uckfield on Saturday to receive their prizes. The following obtained rewards. Note. In consequence of the examination papers not reaching their destination the prizes were awarded before our papers were inspected, those children whose papers were deemed sufficiently good received prizes.

Fred. Waldock	1st Writing, 2nd History, 2nd Grammar, 3rd Dictation, 3rd Composition
Annie Sinden	2nd Composition, 3rd Scripture, 3rd Writing, 3rd Dictation.
Elizabeth Hancock	1st Cutting out and making shirt, 2nd Geography

Albert Hall	3rd Writing.
Mary Russell	2nd Making Flannel Garment.
Elizabeth Evenden	1st Hemming Half Handkerchief.
Sarah Parris	1st Reading in lower Standards,
	1st Spelling in lower Standards.

The School received a Certificate for the Best in Writing.

July 27   The School closed on Monday, the Master taking 44 of the inhabitants of this parish to the Crystal Palace…

Aug. 10   Very many of the Children absent employed in the fields gleaning. Allowed Frederick Waldock to do Algebra, in the place of Arithmetic when the latter subject occurs in the Time Table. The Mapping on Monday afternoon was extremely well done.

Aug. 14   The School closed for four weeks. The Holidays have commenced considerably earlier in consequence of the failure of the Hops.

Sept. 21   Attendance improved but still many are absent in the fields. Two children admitted from Waldron, having to walk nearly four miles, besides paying double fees.

Oct. 26   …A holiday was given on Thursday in consequence of a special service being held in the Church on the occasion of the opening of a New organ.

Nov. 2   …Revd. T. Bishopp took Frederick Waldock and James Thurley in Algebra and Euclid…

Nov. 9   …Commenced a Night School, present 18. Four young men over 18 years commenced to learn to read, one family from Ripe and one from Framfield…

Dec. 14   The unusually severe weather and Snow prevented many from attending during the latter part of the week. Owing to the snow being so deep no school was held on Thursday.

Dec. 21   Emma Trill fell in fit, but soon revived. Broke up on Wednesday for Xmas holiday. Weather extremely severe.

1875

Jan. 4   Commenced School after the Xmas Vacation - owing to the bad state of the road after the thaw many children absent.

Jan. 11   The weather still continues very wet. Frederick Waldock and James Thurley examined in Algebra (Simple Equation) and Euclid (First x Prop) by the Revd. T. Bishopp, who awarded 2/6d. to Waldock and gave Thurley 1/- for his diligence.

Feb. 8   Many children who will have to be presented at the government examination absent. Heard that T. P. although having made only a third of his attendances is employed contrary to the Act.

Mar. 15   …Examined First Class in Geography of Europe and Repetition of "The Fall of Wolsey" and "The Last Minstrel". All knew the text, but the expression requires Practise.

May 3   On Wednesday the fourth instant the annual holiday and treat of the children took place, nearly 200 mustered and paraded the village. Owing to the prizes given by the Revd. E. Langdale, Miss Borradaile and Miss Langdale for the best design in Garden and Wild Flowers, the Garlands and Maypole were unusually excellent. By the liberality of the Managers an ample number of admirable prizes were given to the most successful children during the last year. After a plentiful Tea the children repaired to Mr. Parris' field, where a multitude of amusements were provided by the resident gentry. Three hearty cheers for the Managers and Secretary of the School terminated an enjoyable day…

May 24   …Alfred Saunders taken ill during the holiday and died of Croup. His sudden death casting a gloom over the School. Sent out to each of the Parents of the children the annual Statement of the Managers.

June 7   Captain Clements visited the school and inspected new boarding put round the room on the previous Saturday. Many of the children are still absent Hop-tying.

June 28   …On Saturday, the 3rd of July the First class were examined by the Revd. E. Langdale and the Revd. T. Bishopp in the Old and New Testament, Catechism and Prayer Book for prizes given by the Chailey Decanal Educational Union. The paper work lasted four hours.

July 5   On Saturday July 10th the First Class were again examined in Writing, Arithmetic, Dictation, Geography, History and Mapping in paperwork.

July 19   …On Saturday the children who were successful in the examinations in the Chailey Education Union to the number of 14 went to Newick to receive their prizes. The following received prizes:

Annie Sinden	1st Writing 5/- 1st Dictation 5/- 3rd Composition 2/- 4th Scripture 2/- 3rd Making Flannel Garment 2/-
Jane Thurley	1st for Writing 5/- 2nd Arithmetic 3/-
Annie Newnham	3rd Arith. 2/- 3rd Mapping 2/- 3rd Making Whole Shirt 2/-
Mary Russell	1st Knitting Silk Stocking 5/-
Emily Hall	1st for Reading under 11 2/6
Sarah Parris	1st Writing on Slates under 11 2/6
Ada Wren	(under 8) 1st Writing on Slates
Jane Whitbourne	2nd for Scripture 5/-
Eliz. Evenden	1st for Stitching
James Thurley	1st for History 5/- 3rd for Scripture 3/-
Frederick T. Jones	(Under 11) 1st Reading 2/6 1st Writing 2/6
Alfred Gifkins	(under 8) 1st for Reading 2/6 2nd for Spelling 1/6 2nd for Writing 1/6

To the Master a certificate for the best school in Reading, Writing and History.

Aug. 9   On Monday afternoon went into school at 1.30 p.m. and dismissed the school at 3.30. In order that the elder girls might go to Miss Borradaile's House to take part in a game of Stool Ball. Harvest operations having become general, a good many children are absent from this Cause.

Aug. 30   Very small school only about 46 present but with the prospect of a long hop picking we are compelled to keep the school on. Broke up on Thursday for the Holidays. Miss Benham, the Infant Mistress resigned after a service of nearly 9 years. She was presented this afternoon with a testimonial of the value of £5 6s. 6d. by the Gentry and inhabitants of Easthothly.

Oct. 10   An extra week was obliged to be given on account of the excessively long Hoppicking…

Nov. 1   Captain Clements visited the school on Friday morning and arranged about the Night School for the ensuing Winter.

Nov. 8   Over 30 absent on Monday morning. The attendance of the Girls is really very serious especially those of the higher standards who require so much more instruction…M. A. W. has been kept at home since August, Harvesting, Hop-picking and now collecting acorns, this last employment has been a great evil this autumn.

Dec. 5   Owing to the violent Snow storm only about a dozen children and <u>two infants</u>! put in an appearance. Sent them Home as soon as the weather moderated. Only 41 on Tuesday morning.

1876

Feb. 7   Dismissed a boy W. C. for using bad language…

Feb. 14   Received a note from C., Chiddingly begging me to re-admit his son as he was excessively sorry for his mis-conduct, and he had punished him severely. Allowed the boy to come again on the distinct understanding that the first time he transgresses he will be dismissed. Weather Wet.

Mar. 6   Measles is increasing alarmingly. Thirty are absent from this cause. Every child from the Nursery is absent through this epidemic, and now it has appeared in the Village…

Mar. 13   Forty-eight absent. Thirty seven cases of Measles. Gave notice that those children whose parents were anxious about their children catching it had better keep them at home for a while. The only chance of keeping a school is receiving those children who have recovered, or who have had it.

Mar. 20   The Infant School was closed for a week in consequence of the measles being so very prevalent. Nearly 50 absent in this room from the same cause…

Apr. 10   The weather during the week has been unusually severe. Several terrific snowstorms preventing the distant children from attending. Friday being the anniversary of our Lords crucifixion, no school was held.

Apr. 28   The older children commenced the History and Grammar for the next year.

May 2   The School treat took place. Two hundred and twenty children were regaled with an abundant supply of excellent cake and tea, after the usual march through the village. Notwithstanding the excessively backward spring the garlands were very good. Captain Clements and the Revd. E. Langdale distributed prizes to those children who had been successful in Needlework, Home Lessons, etc.

May 15   Attendance very good, obliged to refuse three from Chiddingly who applied for admission, on the ground of insufficient space.

June 26   The School examined from 9.30 to 1 by the Revd. Robert Blight Diocesan Inspector. The Children were examined in Scripture, Catechism and Liturgy. Ten were awarded certificates of Merit, viz. James Thurley, E. J. Thurley, Frederick T. Jones, Annie Parris, Alfred Gifkins, William Lock, Emily Saunders, Phoebe Turner, Annie Thurley and Elizabeth Durrant.

July 3   William J. Hancock absent during the week, having to attend the Scholarship Examination at Battersea Training College. On Saturday the First Class were examined on paper in Church History, Geography, Scripture Geography, History Grammar, Arithmetic and Composition. The Revd. E. Langdale and the Rev. T. Bishopp conducted the examination. On Wednesday evening the Sunday School children were examined in Holy Scripture on paper. Miss Borradaile conducting the inspection. The Revd. E. Langdale and the Revd. T. Bishopp inspected the first class on Saturday morning in Religious Knowledge. The examination questions sent by the Diocesan Inspector. Four papers of one hour each were set on Old Testament History, New Testament Liturgy and Catechism. With the exception of the Old Testament they were exceptionally difficult.

July 17   The average for the week has been 97.6. The heat has been 127 in the Sun and 81 in the shade, considering this tropical heat the children have done a fair amount of work.

July 24   Received list of prizes awarded to the successful children in connection with the Chailey Education Union.

1st for Composition	5/-	James Thurley
1st for Prayer Book	7/6	James Thurley
1st for Geography	5/-	Frederick T. Jones
1st for Arithmetic	5/-	Eliz. Evenden
2nd for Arithmetic	3/-	Jane Thurley
2nd for Geography	3/-	Eliz. Evenden
3rd for Geography	2/-	Jane Thurley
3rd for Scripture	3/-	Phoebe Turner
4th for Scripture	2/-	James Thurley

Boys under 8:

2nd for Scripture	3/-	Albert E. Turner

To the Master for best school in the Deanery for Arithmetic and Geography.

Aug. 1   On Wednesday the master was summoned to the bedside of his father, by telegram. His parent expired on Saturday.

Aug. 14   The weather so intensely hot, it required a great amount of exertion to make the children work. Several absent gleaning. In consequence of the small prospect of a good hop-picking the School will break up a fortnight earlier.

Oct. 16   …Had to caution several against coming late. The T.'s and G.'s often coming in a few minutes after two o.c. and consequently losing their mark. I purpose after the new clock, which arrived on the 19th is fixed to close the School doors at 2 o.c…

Oct. 30 …I have been obliged to refuse applications for admittance. Numbers from Chiddingly would like to come if we had accommodation with the exception of 8 or 10 all reside in the parish.

Nov. 6 Having occasion to bring S. P. & A. J. out of the class, Mrs. J. kept the whole of the children away for the afternoon, as this practise had been previously adopted by Mrs. H. in revenge for her girls staying in, I sent the following letter to Mr. J.

Dear Sir,

In consequence of the excessive irregularity of your children, combined with the present motive for their withdrawal from School, I am reluctantly compelled to dismiss them.

Unless the parents will assist the master in upholding necessary discipline, all instruction will cease to be effective. Mrs. J.'s remarks to S. P. was tantamount to encouraging your children in insubordination. You must see the necessity of my having power to inflict needful correction.

I have no fault to find with the general behaviour of your children but if occasion requires as it did yesterday that one should be punished, I will insist on doing so if they attend school.

F. J.

1877

Jan. 1 One of the most terrific hurricanes ever experienced in the South of England. R. Parris one of the boys in Infant School dashed to the ground with sufficient violence to cause him to bleed at the nose. Wednesday a very wet day.

This storm not only damaged one of the little infants, but it caused the collapse of Eastbourne's pier which had been open for five years, and had withstood some very heavy seas without previous mishap.

Jan. 21 Cover-beating has this year assumed a new character, and become a great evil. From a dozen to twenty boys being weekly, and occasionally oftener, absent from this cause. As only the older boys are required this is excessively hurtful to the School.

Feb. 5 …Examined Frederick Jones, William Reid, Alexander Reid and Luther Breeze in First 15 props. in Euclid. Algebra to Simple Equations, and Latin Grammar. Alex Reid the best in Euclid. F. T. Jones in Latin.

Mar. 5 …C. G. away, employed by Dr. Holman this is a direct violation of the act which came into operation at the commencement of the year. T. T. and his sister absent, playing about at home!

In 1876 the Government passed the Elementary Education Act, which required every child between the ages of 5 and 11 to stay at school to be taught the three Rs, and it required the parents to ensure their children attended school. Until this act was passed there was no compulsion for children to be educated and it was only those who wished to do so sent their children to school and paid a small fee. For the next twenty years schooling, and the fee, were compulsory.

A School Attendance Committee was formed and Mr. Charles Brooker was appointed attendance officer for an area centred on Uckfield. He had the authority to bring offending parents before the magistrates. No child between the ages of ten and fourteen could be employed without a certificate of education proficiency. In East Hoathly, no child between ten and thirteen could be employed unless he had made at least 250 attendances in the course of the year, and he had also passed an examination for a Certificate of Exemption. If he met these requirements he was issued with a Labour Certificate and allowed to work. All East Hoathly children went to Uckfield for this test.

Mar. 26   <u>Scarlet fever</u> broke out in the School on Thursday last. Three of Robert Parris' Children failed with it. The rest of the family were carrying the infection about the parish. Clara Parris was attending School on Thursday. Medical men ought to prohibit children from attending a public school on the first symptoms of an infectious disease, and the parents who wilfully disobey such prohibition, ought to be severely censured, in public.

On December 17th 1877 Mr. Avis, the Sanitary Inspector, recommended that children who had come into contact with scarlet fever should not be allowed to attend school. Until this time there had been no such regulation, and epidemics of measles, scarlet fever, diphtheria, mumps etc. swept through the school and village with great rapidity.

The head had done his best in previous years by warning parents of illness in the school, but many appeared to send their children regardless of the state of their health. Because of the crowded conditions of the school there is little wonder that disease spread so rapidly.

On June 10, 1888, there is the first entry mentioning Dr. E. F. Fussell, the Sanitary Inspector, when he inspects the school and orders it to be closed because of Diphtheria - a highly infectious disease, spread by coughing, sneezing, etc. This is the first time something positive is done to combat these epidemics - inoculations against the diphtheria are first mentioned at the school in 1941.

May 1   The annual treat was given to the children. About 196 were present. A splendid variety of Books were awarded to those children who by their success at Government Examination showed their diligence during the past year. Captain Clements and the Revd. E. Langdale gave the books to the recipients.

May 7   Received from the Infant Room 18 children. The Reading very fair and the Writing good. H. S. dismissed for using bad language.

June 11   …A committee meeting was held at the Rectory, to endeavour to provide extra accommodation, the numbers being excessive. The School was inspected on Friday the 15th of June by the Revd. Robert Blight. 17 children were awarded certificates, being an increase of seven over last year.

June 25   Received a visit from Captain Clements and C. Borradaile Esq. to select a situation for proposed New Infant School.

July 23   …On Wednesday the children were presented with 3d. each on the occasion of the wedding of Henry Langdale, Esq.

Aug. 13   The Scarlet Fever broke out in the Nursery…

Oct. 15   Very large School. Obliged to slightly modify the Time table by working the first and second classes as the First class. Average for the past week 123.5 being the highest since the School was opened.

Dec. 10   …On Saturday, the Revd. Sutton Leach and Soale inspected the proposed site of the New Infants School.

Dec. 17   Elizabeth Howell failed with the Fever, Annie Sinden the Paid Monitor consequently compelled to be absent. The Bentleys, Tucks and Berrys ill with the same. Mr. Avis the sanitary inspector wrote to say that the children in the same house with those having the fever were not to [be] allowed to attend, of course this had previously been insisted upon.

1878

Jan. 14   Mr. Thomas Holman Surgeon of East Hothly called at the School and ordered the whole of the children in the district of the Nursery to be kept at home in consequence of a serious outbreak of Scarlet Fever. Five families infected. Mr. George Bentley has no less than seven of the inmates of his house down with it at once. Received from Captain Clements a letter, giving his sanction to the above order. This necessitates the withdrawal of about 40 children.

Jan. 21   Two boys named Gladman failed with the Fever having only attended school a few days. Received a communication from H. Jones, Esq., Clerk to the School Attendance Committee of the Uckfield Union, intimating that after the 1st of January the Committee will furnish the necessary Child's School Book free of cost. That the Superintendent Registrar of Uckfield has consented to accept 3d. for each certificate to be issued by him in respect of children born within his district, but in all other cases a sum of 6d. that being the sum fixed by the provision of the Education Act 1876, should be forwarded to another Superintendent Registrar. In both cases a postage stamp of 1d. should also be sent, if the application for the Certificate is not made personally.

Feb. 11   Another case of Fever in the Infant Room. Eighty three children in the Mixed school and 37 in the Infant Room absent through sickness. On Thursday morning only 32 present and in the afternoon 36. The absent children are away with whooping cough and Scarlet Fever.

Mar. 11   The children continue excessively sickly. Several that attend school owing to the severeness of the hooping cough are unable to do their work.

June 3   …Frederick Jones, Master of Easthothly National School received his Certificate from the Education Department conveying the notification that the certificate was raised to the First Class…

June 24   On Wednesday and Thursday a holiday was given, Miss Laura Langdale, the daughter of our esteemed Rector, having been married to G. Trist Esq. The wedding breakfast took place in the School Room.

July 1   The Infant School occupied their New Room. The

buildings were planned by the master of the Mixed School and built by Richard Hall under the Superintendence of the Secretary of the Schools, Captain Clements. The order and discipline of the Mixed School vastly improved, with the increased space afforded by an additional class room, the teachers were enabled to work without the noise, which had previously been utterly impossible to avoid.

July 8   On Friday the annual treat which had been pos[t]poned to await the opening of the Infant School took place. The New School was opened with a service of divine prayer conducted by the Revd. Edward Langdale. About 250 children were provided with a liberal supply of eatables on the lawn in front of the Rectory. Amongst the company present besides most of the resident gentry were L. Huth, Esq., Sir Edmund Hornby, Revd. J. Ley, Rev. Henry Geldart and Co. After the comestibles had vanished, Captain Clements distributed the prizes to those children who had passed a good examination at the Government Inspection and whose conduct had been satisfactory during the Year. The three children to whom "Honour Certificates" had been present by H.M.I. received the whole of their school pence for the past year.

July 29   …F. and W. W. cautioned as to their future conduct, having been repeatedly punished for using bad language and stone throwing. A repetition of such gross misconduct will result in their dismissal by the managers. I am afraid that Home influence and example counteracts the good inculcated at School.

Aug. 19   …The new fence constructed of Brick Piers and iron fencing completed.

Oct. 14   Large number present on Monday. Examined the children admitted from the Infant School and found them excessively backward, that I despair of getting them up to the required pitch. The Reading is disgraceful in the majority of cases, this is no fault of the Infant Mistress, as most of the children had only been present in the Infant School in all probability for a few months. The dame schools are the bane of education, a great number of the children admitted from Mrs. Thorps School at the Nursery have been there for several years, and then seek admission to the National School, when the Master is obliged to do the work of the Infant teachers, with no prospect of the children passing the Government Examination, the Master consequently receiving no credit for his exertions, as the majority of such children must inevitably fail.

Nov. 4   Tuesday being the anniversary of Gunpowder plot, many of the boys made this an excuse for being absent. The Home Lessons better done than in the previous week. By giving marks for the work done and publishing a weekly class list, which determines the position of each child for the ensuing week many whose parents are against this work are reluctantly compelled to do it in order to maintain their position in their class.

Nov. 11   …H. W. excessively troublesome, using bad language this is a case where dismissal is the lesser evil, one thorough bad boy is a contamination to the whole school. A little boy in the First standard got into sad disgrace through the tutorage of W.

Nov. 18   Several children absent with severe croupy colds…Gave the First class on Wednesday a description of Afghanistan, the causes which led to the present complication with a brief account of the chief points to be attacked by the invading army.

1879

Jan 6   The weather during the past week was unusually severe, the frost being intense…Mr. Brooker received a list of 65 children who had been irregular during the previous 9 months, with number of attendances that each child ought to make in order to be examined.

Jan. 27   118 present on Monday morning. Several returned after an extremely long absence. The master had the agreeable task of complimenting E. Evenden for the admirable manner in which she preserved the discipline of the second Standard. Jane Whitbourne teaches the third standard with considerable skill but is rather inclined to be too lenient. Both have been assiduous.

Feb. 24   Gave the IV, V. and VI Standards the Geography of Natal and Zululand, illustrating on the B. B. the position of the British Forces and the scene of the recent disaster. On Thursday the weather was very severe, snow falling rapidly.

Mar. 16   On Tuesday afternoon 140 children were present. 139 were marked, and E. Gasson came in late. This is the greatest number present at one time since the School has been opened. Frederick Thomas Jones was awarded a certificate by Dr. Macaulay Editor of the Boys Own Paper for excellence in Latin composition.

HUGH GOOLD WEBB
1879-1880

Apr. 21   I, Hugh Goold Webb took charge of and opened this school this morning, attendance 128.

May 2   Have been re-arranging standards and settling to work.

May 13   The first class having been kept in, A. R. was found sitting on the desk, from which position he obstinately refused to move, for which case of insubordinature, aggravated by a previous one, he was expelled the school.

May 14   After a conversation held with Mrs. R., A. R. was taken back to school.

Aug. 8   …A whole holiday was given today on account of the children having their annual School-treat. Over 240 were present, and 49 received prizes. The two principal prizes were received by Edmund and Richard Thatcher for the highest number of attendance, having missed only two and three half days respectively…

1880

Mar. 22   …A letter was received on Thursday from the Clerk of the School Attendance Committee, enclosing forms of certificate of non-attendance at School etc. of J. M. and R. E., for filling to be used as evidence in proceedings taken against their father…

On April 7th Class Subjects are listed and include Geography (Great Britain for Standard 4 and Europe for Standards 5 and 6), Grammar, Physical Geography for the boys and Domestic Economy for the girls, literature, Mathematics, and latin for one boy only; and the literature for 1881 is given as King Robert of Sicily and The Lady of the Lake.

The timetable for 1880-81 makes rather boring reading. The first class had two composition classes a week, one map drawing class, one writing class, one literature class, 8 reading classes, 2 grammar classes, 5 arithmetic classes, 3 geography classes, 2 music classes, 5 phy. geog. and mechanics, and 4 literature. The V class is even worse: 3 lessons in transcription, 8 in reading, 7 in writing, 10 in arithmetic, 2 music and 5 dictation. From 2.30 to 4 o'clock every afternoon the girls had needlework. This is Mr. Webb's new and improved timetable. However in 1884 under Mr. Jones' headship we have the appearance of counting and spelling lessons, natural history, drill, letters, paper pricking followed by embroidery on paper, knitting for boys and girls two afternoons a week, form and colour, object lesson and "unravelling stuff", a lesson called "various occupations" and one Moral Instruction Lesson. Each day finished either with poetry or singing for 10 minutes. The Inspector was unable to report favourably of the school under Mr. Webb, there was "need for much more thoroughness and painstaking care", and a deduction in the Grant would be necessary unless there was considerable improvement.

May 3   …The Attendance Officer called with two certifi. to be filled in and signed as evidence in summonses to be taken against the parents of L. P. and J. E.

May 17   On Thursday the children had a whole holiday on account of the marriage of Miss Rickett; they each had the sum of 6d. given to them, and in the afternoon, marched to Barham, and walked about the grounds.

May 24   …2 doz. inkwells, 2 b.boards and 3 easels were received.

Aug. 26   Mr. Brooker called yesterday to see who had returned to school out of the list given to him last week. The registers were looked over, before him, as he called the names…No fresh names were given him.

Mr. Webb had great trouble with absentees, long lists of names are given to the Attendance Officer. However, on Mr. Jones' return in November, the attendance gradually began to improve. The standard of teaching declined under Mr. Webb and it took all Mr. Jones' efforts to bring the school up to its original excellence. The Inspector's report regretted the decline in efficiency under Mr. Webb but registered the confidence that the position would certainly improve under the renewed headship of Mr. Jones.

Nov. 8   The new Master, Frederick Jones, resumed his duties at his old sphere of labour. Found the condition of the school simply deplorable. The condition of the School material, in a disgraceful state. Before commencing duties the Master and Pupil-Teachers cleansed the Desks and Offices. The children are sadly behind, the first class being unable to do any of the arithmetic, or extra subjects for the ensuing year. In an examination of the 4th and 3rd standards, no child had less than three mistakes several over 12. The arithmetic is also extremely bad…

Nov. 15   The master has during the week examined the whole school so as to ascertain the capabilities of each individual child and to infuse a little more vigour into the teaching of the pupil teachers which has become somewhat lax through want of supervision…

Nov. 24   The average for the week has been 110.8. The master had to caution the boys against swearing, and the want of respect to their superiors. The Police Sergeant visited the School on Friday and complained of the behaviour of the boys in trespassing over hedges and fences, this want of order out of School is a serious evil, and will receive my utmost attention, the necessity of supervision in the Playground is needed to check the evil; True respect to superiors is the fundamental root of good discipline.

1881

Jan. 17   An unusually severe frost…On Tuesday morning occurred one of the most violent snowstorms experienced by this generation. The children were prevented from coming to school. The snow drifting in some places over five feet. Charles Denman who attended in the afternoon only was prevented from getting home from Uckfield being unable to get further than High Cross. On Wednesday only 24 present, a way having to be dug for them.

Mar. 21   …Examined William Reid in the First and Second Books of Euclid. Robert Reid, Alexander Jones and Alfred Gifkins in the first fifteen propns. in Euclid. The master took Jane Whitburn and Elizabeth Evenden to the Pupil-teachers examinations at the Central Schools Lewes on Saturday the 26th of March.

Apr. 11   The attendance very indifferent, several children have been absent planting potatoes at Whyly Farm, so long as employers of labour escape all the penalties of the Education Act so long will parents be persuaded and in some instances be compelled to break the law.

Apr. 19   A great many children absent without any sufficient cause. The attendance is the one evil which militates against that efficiency which the managers and teachers strive after. The compulsory attendance of the irregular children as carried out by our local attendance committee is a mere farce.

May 16   …On Friday a meeting of the rate-payers was held at the Kings Head Inn, when the advisableness of having a School Board was discussed. It was ultimately decided to increase the Voluntary subscriptions.

June 27   …W. W. was dismissed the School by order of the Secretary, Captain Clements for continued misconduct. This boy has been guilty of stealing flowers from the Church Yard, and money from his parents. As he is habitually punished at home the master tried to win him by kindness instead of corporal punishment, but his case seems hopeless and for the sake of the other children on whom his example was extremely prejudicial his expulsion became a decided necessity.

July 11   …Friday was the annual School treat. Over 250 children were present. The children were presented with a valuable collection of prizes, among those present in addition to the Managers and Secretary of the School were L. Huth, Esq. and J. Rickett, Esq.

The Annual meeting of the Chailey Educational Union took place at Fletching. The successful children in the late examinations were entertained in the grounds of the Rectory and received prizes an address on the present state of Education was delivered by the Revd. Julius Hannah of Brighton. The master of the School received a certificate of Merit for the best School in the Deanery in respect to Bible Knowledge, Catechism, Church History, Scripture Geography, Needlework (above 8 years) and Church singing.

Oct. 3   Commenced School after 5 weeks vacation, the extra week was given in consequence of lateness of the Harvesting and Hoppicking operations which had been delayed by the extreme wetness of the season…

Nov. 21   The weather on Monday morning was extremely violent only 79 present. Gave the School by way of caution a lesson on "Respect due to one-another". The behaviour of several boys both in the Playground and the Village is not all that is to be desired. Occasionally a boy seems to be naturally a bully, I find the great cure is to expose his mean cowardly actions before the whole school, unless this great evil is nipped in the bud the lesser children soon learn to imitate the fault.

Dec. 12   E. G. attended on one day during the week. Her parents openly defy the attendance committee, they have been previously fined on several occasions. In such a case the fine of 5/- is a mere farce…Mr. Booker called on Wednesday when the irregular children were reported.

1882

Jan. 30   On Sunday morning our beloved Rector the Revd. E. Langdale died. The families in the Ivy House kept from school by order of Dr. Holman. The Hutsons, Bookers and Leaders absent from the outbreak of Scarlet Fever. The Gassons and Pages are also forbidden to attend school.

Feb. 13   The parents of E. G. were fined at Uckfield for the irregular attendance of their daughter on Thursday the 16th. T. P. and F. B. will scarcely be able to complete their attendances. F. B.

has never been examined although able to pass the 3rd Standard never having made 250 attendances in one year.

Apr. 24   …Hop tying has commenced this year much earlier owing to the extremely forward Spring. As a consequent result many girls are assisting at home.

May 1   The average greatly reduced by a serious outbreak of hooping cough and measles. Sent five children home on Tuesday having heard that the epidemic was serious, and that the families of the Hunnisetts and Bristows were suffering from it. A number of girls are also assisting at home in consequence of their parents being employed in hop tying…

May 7   School still suffering from epidemics. Measles Scarlet Fever and Hooping cough preventing many children from attending. Elizabeth Evenden returned from the Infants School on Wednesday having conducted that department during the unavoidable absence of the Infant Mistress in a very efficient manner. Special attention has been paid to the Arithmetic during the last week. It is essential to success that whole of the Arithmetic has been taught by the Harvest Holidays so that ample time for practise and coaching backward children may be obtained. Geography is well forward as the First Class studied "Europe" during the previous year in addition to the British Possessions.

June 26   Admitted two children aged 12 and 8 extremely backward. The girl has been attending a dame school at the Nursery, and is quite unable to read the easiest words. She ought to have been attending the Infant School where she would have been able to work with Standard I. Not knowing her letters she cannot work with any class satisfactorily.

July 7   A holiday was given on Friday when the Revd. Harry Harbord was inducted to the living of East Hothly by the Lord Bishop of Chichester.

Aug. 14   Many children employed in harvesting operations especially as there is little prospect of a long hop-picking. The parents being anxious to earn a little extra to provide winter clothing.

Dec. 11   The snow has prevented many children from attending. No less than three children taken ill at School, the foggy weather combined with large attendances being no doubt the cause.

1883

Feb. 12   The average for the week was considerably reduced by the rain, the children who live at a distance have been wet through almost every night but notwithstanding the health of the children is very good. The boy C. is very irregular suffering from Kings Evil, for a portion of the time he has attended during the year, he was suffering from this dreadful complaint, having a large hole under his chin.

King's Evil is an old name for Scrofula, which is a tubercular disease of the lymphatic glands. It was believed that it could be cured by the touch of a King's hand - hence the name. It was not a particularly dangerous disease, many cases recovering fully, but others could develop

T.B. elsewhere. The hole referred to in this child's neck would appear to be the result of the "cold abscess" which would have formed, leaving ulcers and unsightly scars.

Mar. 26   School kept open on Easter Monday in order that several of the children may complete their attendances. Several children run extremely close, the master having to send home urgent notices to the parents to keep the children at school every day.

Apr. 16   Lord Pelham of Stanmer Park sent a present of oranges for the children, which were distributed on Wednesday.

Apr. 23   Admitted 2 children from Laughton School both exceedingly backward and had not been examined in any standard and one from Blackboys N.S. who had passed the First Standard.

Apr. 25   Lord Pelham sent a second quantity of oranges for distribution amongst the children making 700 received altogether. This liberal present afforded immense gratification to the boys and girls.

Apr. 30   …On Tuesday the Revd. Harry Harbord communicated to the teachers the welcomed intelligence that he had received a notification from the patron of the living that he would hold the office of pastor of the parish for a permanency. On Wednesday, Mrs. E. Langdale the relic of our late beloved rector was interred beside her departed husband. The School children prepared a wreath for her grave.

May 21   …The parting wall between the original infant School and the Mixed Department was removed making one room 48 feet 6 in. long. The school worked a little out of groove in consequence but soon settled down to its accustomed routine. A slight echo is detected and the alteration produces a reverberation…

May 28   …The beautiful rain on Saturday has made the farmers very busy with their hops, and many children are pressed into their service completing the tying. The hops are the cause of a deal of absenteeism on the part of the pupils of this school; when mothers are in the gardens the children are invariably away.

June 25   …The Revd. H. Harbord and Captain Clements visited the School on Friday morning and informed the master that the usual treat would take place in July and that the excessively irregular children were to be kept away.

July 16   On Friday a treat was given to the children at Fir-grove by the Managers, including the Sunday scholars about 270 children were present and spent an enjoyable afternoon.

Aug. 20   …The foundation stone of the new rectory was laid on Monday by the Marchioness of Abergavenny…

Oct. 29   …The master gave attention to the Arith: of the Upper standards, teaching Compound Proportion and Percentages.

1884

Jan. 7   …Gave examination to the whole school. The first standard requires most attention. The three children admitted at the commencement of this quarter excessively backward, A. A. unable to point out the letters of the alphabet. During the week the backward portion of this Standard go into my house to be coached by Mrs. Jones.

Jan. 14   On Tuesday Evening a lecture was given in the School Room illustrated with dissolving views, by lime light by Compton Rickett, Esq. No School in the afternoon.

Compton Rickett was the eldest son of the Squire of Barham House. The lecture was entitled "Old England and A Race around the World". "The scenes depicted were produced by lime light and the apparatus was "of a powerful character". Realistic pictures of ancient British history together with vivid representation of geographical interest were produced with distinctness and photographic accuracy…The lecture was delivered in a fluent and graphic manner and gave great satisfaction". The audience numbered 230 persons, a very pleasing turnout!

Feb. 11   …The chicken pox is very prevalent in the school, the teachers are obliged to exercise great care to stop the infection.

Feb. 25   The attendance during the week was very good most of the children who have been ill have returned, though several seem to suffer from debility. I find that the recreation at 10.30 has a great influence on the health of the school in continued wet weather when the children are unable to obtain fresh air the classes seem to suffer from lassitude and that brightness is absent, which is indicative of mental activity.

Apr. 4   Lord Pelham sent from Lewes, a present of 600 oranges, to be given to the children.

The pages for April 4th 1884 to May 5th 1886 are missing.

On July 4th 1884 the Infants Log Book gives a list of natural history object lessons for the Infants as below:

List of Natural History Object Lessons, Etc.

1. Tea	1. Elephant
2. Sugar	2. Whale
3. Leather	3. Cow
4. Soap	4. Goose
5. Paper	5. Lion
6. Glass	6. Swan
7. Silk	7. Butterfly
8. Wheat	8. Donkey
9. Coffee	9. Goldfinch
10. Water	10. Beaver
11. Hop-picking	11. Dog.
12. Fruit and Flowers	12. Birds and Beasts.
Gentleness	The Human Ear
Kindness to Animals	The Human Hand
Stealing	The Human Eye
Throwing Stones	The Human Face.
Politeness	

1886

June 21   The attendance was very good except on the fete day at Laughton when Sir James Duke came of age.

From the report in the local paper, this was a very grand affair involving almost everyone in the area. There were several marquees, the ballroom marquee being 100 foot long and 40 foot wide, "lined in crimson and white and with tasselled cordons", 7 chandeliers of 30 lights each and wall lights. The supper marquee was about half this size, and 400 tenants and friends attended, the festivities beginning at 9 o'clock in the evening and ending at 4 in the morning when photographs were taken on the lawn.

June 28   …Haymaking has now become general, and the parents are only too pleased to allow every available child to earn a small sum…In the afternoon of the same day the annual treat took place in the grounds of the Rectory. The delightful weather enabled the children to pass a most enjoyable afternoon. On Friday the attendance was extremely bad many thinking that a holiday was given.

July 5   On Thursday the 8th there was no school, the General Election taking place, the school being used as a Polling Station.

Aug. 2   …The harvest is this year very backward, parents are anxious to get their children employed on every available opportunity. This school has for twenty years worked steadily, as a consequence children pass the 4th standard at eleven years of age with few exceptions. It is a bitter disappointment to teachers to find that some dozen or more girls too young for service are parading the street early with perambulators learning habits of laziness and undoing the good acquired at School. Even master tradesmen are now taking away their boys as soon as they have fulfilled the requirements of the law. The Fifth Standard ought to be the lowest that a child should pass before leaving.

Aug. 16   …Several parents have asked permission for their boys to go to work till after hop-picking leave has been granted in every instance…

Aug. 23   …Frederick Thomas Jones A.M. received a letter from the Secretary of the Brighton School of Science and Art, stating the result of his recent examinations, Certificates were awarded for success in Agriculture, Physiography, Freehand and Geometry…

1887

Jan. 24   …Two girls late and lost their mark. Both punished by being kept in during the whole of the dinner time.

Mar. 21   …The mother of the B.'s stated that they had both passed the second standard as they were excessively backward and not capable of doing the work of the First Standard, the master sent to Laughton, when the Master of Laughton B.S. reported that they had never been presented in any standard. Mr. Jackson, the Master of Ringmer B.S. stated in his note that they had attended the Board School in the parish of Ringmer for 9 months, were excessively backward and left the parish about four months before their examination. Transferred them to the First Standard in the Infant School.

Apr. 18   A. R. one of the sixth standard girls is away shaving hop-poles, she ought to be present, the excuse is that her father is unable to stoop and she is obliged to assist him.

May 16   A great many children who have satisfied the Government requirement by passing the Fourth Standard have left. In schools similar to this one where a good infant department exists, the period of exemption is arrived at too soon, and children are free and do leave before they can procure employment, the consequence is that they are in the street acquiring habits of laziness etc. and undoing the good previously inculcated. No child ought to leave before they pass the fifth standard if under 11 years when the fourth standard is passed…

June 6   …Learnt the children several songs to sing on the occasion of the Jubilee of Her Most Gracious Majesty the Queen. Thursday was the anniversary of the Calvanistic denomination and many children were away in the afternoon from this cause. Anniversaries and clubs are the bane of a teachers life and are the means of instilling habits of laziness and love of pleasure.

June 20   No school on Monday, Tuesday and Wednesday. On Tuesday the whole of the parish was entertained at Barham by J. Rickett, Esq. being the occasion of the celebration of the Jubilee of Her Majesty the Queen. Every variety of amusement was provided in addition to a public dinner and tea; the weather was delightful and the conduct of the public admirable. The total absence of all drunkenness and coarse or profane language, combined with the well behaved conduct of every one can only be attributed to the increase of knowledge and spread of education.

On the 27th June 1887 Miss Rhoda Wenham "lately Asst. Mistress Chiddingly Board School," commenced her Duties as Assistant and Sewing Mistress in the School and so began another long association with the school, Miss Wenham finally retiring in March 1929 for family reasons.

July 18   The C.'s have taken no notice of the repeated warnings of the attendance officer. The master went and saw the father who laid the blame on the mother and promised that they should attend more regularly this promise has not been kept.

Aug. 1   …Punished F. R. for indecent language to a little girl in the same class. As this abominable crime is of very rare occurrence, I took him before the Rector, before administering punishment and he received six stripes in his presence.

Sept. 19   Commenced school after the Summer vacation only four weeks given, there being a small quantity of hops - 99 present on Monday morning. Several children have removed from the parish. The present condition of agriculture causes a considerable amount of migration amongst the labouring population, the farmers employing no more hands than they can possibly help.

Dec. 12   …On Thursday afternoon the whole school was dismissed a little before time to welcome Captain Clements the Secretary on his return to the village after his wedding trip. The inhabitants drew his carriage through the village amid general rejoicing.

Captain Clements' first wife, Caroline Sarah, had died on the 11th April 1886, aged 53. He married Sophia Borrodaile, the elder daughter of the late Rev. Frederick Borrodaile of Heasmonds on the 9th December 1887 at St. Georges, Hannover Square. On the couple's return to East Hoathly, they found that South Street was decorated with flags and crowded with people. When the carriage arrived at Park Lodge, the horse was removed and several villagers pulled the carriage to Belmont, the villagers cheering all the way. The church bells rang and "the blacksmiths fired their anvils". This report more than anything else conveys the feelings of the inhabitants of East Hoathly for Captain Clements and also for Miss Sophia, who had been a great help in teaching the children from the opening days of the school.

1888

Jan. 2   Commenced work again after the Xmas Vacation. Let the children out on Wednesday evening at a quarter to four, the school room being required for a concert, in aid of the School funds.

In the middle of June 1882 the Rev. Harry Harbord had married Miss Ellen Jane, third daughter of Mrs. Blair of Finchcocks Park, Goudhurst. The new Mrs. Harbord wasted no time in organising a Glee Club. Their first concert is reported on the 9th February 1883 and was very well received in the village. They gave another concert in April when much improvement was noticed, and the winter concert appears to have become an annual event, receiving a great deal of support. At one concert, there was not enough room for all those who wished to attend, the overflow standing outside in "inclement weather" and watching through the windows.

Jan. 9   Gave the school a searching examination…The sixth standard boys are an unusually undergrown dull set and require extra attention. It is a curious but a remarkable fact that up to thirteen years the intellect of the girls is in advance of the boys and they are far more apt at their work not excepting Arithmetic.

Jan. 16   …The school is suffering from an epidemic of croup…

Jan. 31   Received a note from Mr. Theakstone (Waldron) stating that a fifth boy named T. would probably apply for admission having got in arrears with school pence. Received also a note from Mr. Gilbert (Laughton) stating that a girl of the name of M. purposed applying for admission having been punished at Laughton S. for stealing wool, as in both cases their excuses for leaving are breaches of discipline, I shall refuse to admit them.

Feb. 20   The ground still covered with snow. Altered the time of work during the afternoon commencing school at 1.30 and closing at 3.30 during the time the snow is melting, as the feet of the children are continually wet. On Tuesday and Friday the children were fed with good hot soup by the Rector. Mrs. Harbord assisted the Teachers in attending to the wants of the children. Owing to the general want of work, many of the children were getting very pinched and feeble the providing of a good hot meal has a great influence in promoting the general health of the children.

Mar. 5   …The children still receive a soup dinner on Tuesdays and Fridays, as there has been more distress in the parish than has been known for many years, this boon has had a very beneficial effect, and has tended to promote the healthiness of the children.

Because of lack of work in the village and the bad weather the children were suffering, and it was decided to provide them with soup. Soup dinners continued for several years, being given free to those whose parents were out of work and a charge of a penny ha'penny made to those who could afford it.

Apr. 16   E. P. sent to school again, without her school fees. The Guardians have refused to pay the fees of poor children in this parish, at a Vestry Meeting on the 25th March the Master brought this subject before the Ratepayers and the Rector was requested to write to the Chairman of the Guardians and strongly urge the necessity of the payment of the fees of several poor families, who for months and in one or two cases for years have been unable to pay their school fees.

June 10   Dr. E. F. Fussell inspected the School on Monday and ordered it to be closed for a fortnight as there were several cases of Diphtheria. Received a letter from Dr. Fussell on Monday June 25th…stating that care must be taken with the childrens clothing. "The hats etc. must be kept separate from each other as much as possible and Lobby door open, especially the girls."

July 9   The Ringworm has followed the Diphtheria…The School ought really to have been closed for a longer time.

July 16   Ringworm and Diphtheria still reduces the average very considerably. Several cases have occurred at the Nursery and Davis Town. The Sanitary Inspector again visited the school. He stated that he was sorry he had not closed the Schools for a longer period. The weather has been very wet and cold more like October than July. Colds have consequently been very prevalent.

Aug. 6   Several changes of farms in the neighbourhood causes a migration of labourers and consequently several children have left the parish. The harvest owing to the wet July is very backward and haying is not finished.

Aug. 13   …A meeting in the School Room on Wednesday at 12 o.c. to decide on tenders for new wall to the proposed addition to the Church Yard, a slight readjustment of the School play ground is contemplated.

Nov. 5   The new addition to the Church Yard was consecrated on Monday afternoon. As the clergy robed in the School Room a half holiday was given. On Tuesday morning the Lord Bishop of Chichester visited the school during the time of religious instruction, the Bishop asked for some texts on the Gloria in Excelsis (the subject the children were receiving a class lesson on) and his Lordship expressed his satisfaction with the childrens answers.

Dec. 3   …The measles are now general and especially bad at the Nursery. The school has suffered this year more from epidemics diphtheria (two outbreaks) ringworm and measles, than I ever remember during the time I have resided at East Hoathly, viz. since 1871.

1889

Jan. 7   …The children who have had the measles are left very sickly and several have to be sent home daily.

Jan. 14   The measles have broken out again very badly several grown up people are ill. Dr. H. C. Holman has ten of his children sick…

Jan. 28   Charles Parris came to school with the Measles out on him and had to send him home…The children who have had the measles are suffering with inflammation in the eyes. Cottingham was sent home as it was cruelty to allow him to work. Lucy French who had suffered with inflammation of the eyes died on Saturday.

Feb. 25   On Saturday the schools were used for the election of County councillors. J. Rickett, Esq. one of the Managers was defeated by Mr. Taylor of Mayfield by 115 votes…

Apr. 15   Gave all the school a searching examination. The fifth standard boys are an exceptionally dull class with few exceptions and although they have received the lion share of attention they are still backward.

Apr. 22   Gave extra attention to Music and Repetition. Examined the whole school again. The weather is the cause of considerable sickness, severe colds and sore throats are very prevalent, in spite of these drawbacks the children have attended whenever possible.

May 20   …The heat on Thursday and Friday was quite extraordinary, 77F. being registered in the schoolroom on Friday with all the blinds down…

May 27   …Several girls commenced the needlework intended for competition at the Flower Show in August.

July 8   …The Master has given objects lessons on Cotton, Sugar, The Elephant, Black Hole of Calcutta and Life of Wellington to assist the composition, and to train the mental faculties.

Aug. 5   …Mary Bentley was selected by all the children for the prize awarded by the Master for Good Conduct during the past year. The School treat took place at Barham on Friday, unfortunately the weather was very wet.

Oct. 6   …The whole of the week was extremely wet. 10 of the Nursery children came in on Friday morning one minute before time and so saved their mark. I had to excuse them as they were wet through the previous evening.

Oct. 13   Punished E. P. and P. H. for destroying school material on Sunday. They were caught swinging the Maps etc…

Dec. 2   Several cases of ringworm. Punished severely G. R. for interfering with A. A. on the way to school. The master spent a great portion of the Dinner recess in the playground with the boys in order to counteract a certain amount of bullying which had lately become fashionable with several of the bigger boys. E. Funnell and Frank Thatcher wrote the best account of the Spanish Armada on Wednesday.

Dec. 9   Gave extra attention to Geography. Showed photo of Scotch scenery and illustrations of the physical features of Australia during class lessons. Country children are at a great disadvantage as they never see the illustrated papers. To endeavour to remedy this want, the Master has obtained illustrated guides as the 'Orient' etc. and Australian catalogues as that of Chaffey Bros. The latter contain magnificent scenes and landscapes giving correct ideas.

1890

Jan. 20   Many of the children returned to school, but very feeble. Several still very ill. The Managers generously supplied them with two good meals on Tuesday and Friday. Mrs. Harbord attended the school from 12 to 12.45 and superintended the distribution, and assisted the teachers in ministering to the childrens wants.

Feb. 10   Miss R. Wenham away from school. Fred. Thomas Jones assisted till Friday when he was obliged to go to bed, with the prevailing sickness. Soup was given on Tuesday and Friday. With the present unhealthy condition of the children and teachers it is almost an impossibility to accomplish the required amount of work.

Feb. 17   Many of the children still away ill…Over hundred stayed to dinner on Tuesday and Friday when soup was distributed. The children as a whole are very sickly.

Apr. 7   Easter Monday…Gave the Boys an extra halfhour Map drawing for attending on Bank Holiday…

June 19   The hay making season has now commenced, and many children are away from this cause. Object lessons were given on Copper and India-rubber. Illustrations and specimens were used, as many as were available. Country children are at a considerable disadvantage in not being able to visit towns where their powers of observation are exercised and considerably developed. Rural-teachers have to turn to what is probably the best school for developing these powers, to nature, but they feel that while they are benefiting the mental faculties of their pupils, they are not doing much for the only standard by which their work is estimated viz. the ensuing Government Inspection.

Aug. 11   …Punished several children on Thursday morning for disobedience. They had been repeatedly warned about careless writing in the Composition Exercise, but no heed was taken, the consequence was strong measures had to be used. Several boys received two stripes in each hand and three girls three stripes.

Aug. 18   …Gave a lesson on the Horse and the Ox. Extra time was given to Musical Drill. Gave a searching examination in Arithmetic. Several problems not done well. Extra time must be given to mental arithmetic. The Master prepared a typical number of problems, these will form the models on which the mental exercises will be given. The wet summer has delayed all farming operations and extended them considerably over the normal time, consequently most of the older children have been more or less irregular and this time of irregularity has been longer than usual.

Nov. 10   …Punished F. H. for hitting a little boy, several of the Nursery boys are guilty of ill-using the little ones…

Nov. 17   Gave an examination of the whole school. The result of putting twelve of the brightest children up two standards in a year is to apparently lower the results. Those children who are put up often form the bottom of the new Standard in which they have been placed, whilst they formed the brightest children in their old standard.

Dec. 1   …S. Trill, Frank and Bertie Thatcher brought very good Freehand drawing for homework. The Homework being voluntary is not so general as one would desire. Henry Holman Esq. who has been a Manager of these Schools for the last twentyfive years viz. from the first building, died on Friday. The decease[d] whose genial manner with the teachers and children rendered him much respected will be greatly missed.

Dec. 8   Funeral of Dr. Holman. Examined the whole school. After working very hard during the last quarter with the T. from the Nursery and E. B. , I find it impossible to get them to do one sum. As there is a taint of imbecility in both cases I can only attribute my discomfiture to this cause.

1891

Jan. 5   The severe cold considerably effects the average. The upper part of the school has been so excessively cold that the children have been quite unable to do paper work for several weeks. The usual work has had to be done on slates.

Jan. 12   Still very cold. The ice on the Decoy Pond is now eight inches thick. On Wednesday afternoon the prizes given at the Baptist Sunday School were given away. Many children absent. The weather is still intensely cold and tends to lower the average. The wall on the side of the School room adjacent the Infant School ought to have a fire-place made in it. The upper part of the room has been so excessively cold that the children could not properly work in that portion. On Friday 128 children had a soup dinner. Nothing tends so much towards promoting the health of the children as a good meat and vegetable dinner, many of the little ones when work is scarce rarely getting more than bread and an apology for butter.

Jan. 19   Very cold morning the children had drill instead of drawing…Frederick Hunnisett found a purse with 5/6 in it. He brought it to the Head teacher who soon found the owner. The owner gave him a penny. The master in order to take advantage of the opportunity commended him before the whole School and gave him a new book not as a reward for honesty, as that he impressed on the boys was their duty, but to show that the Master appreciated the moral rectitude of the lad.

Jan. 26   Soup given out on Tuesday and Friday about 120 at dinner. The Interest, which had previously been reasoned out, taught by formulae. As it would be unwise of my successor to change horses while crossing the stream I enter the following method.

$$As \quad I = \frac{P \times R \times T}{100} \qquad R = \frac{100 \times I}{P \times T}$$

$$T = \frac{100 \times I}{P \times R} \qquad P = \frac{100 \times I}{R \times T}$$

March 9   …In the afternoon a terrific snowstorm commenced, and the children from a distance were sent home at a quarter to 4 o.c. The storm continued with great violence throughout the night and the next day the roads were impassable in many places owing to the drifts often 8 ft. high. No school on Tuesday and Wednesday. Only 62 on Thursday morning.

This snow storm, ten years after the last bad blizzard, caused much havoc on land and the loss of life at sea. It began in the morning of the 9th March and lasted until the 13th March.

Mar. 16   …Owing to mental defects the families of B. and T. have always failed in arithmetic. The master has given these children extra time and attention but when nervous they invariably fail. M. T., S. T. and E. B. have never yet passed in Arithmetic. They are fairly sharp in Reading etc.

Mar. 23   …On Tuesday Evening the Rector addressed the boys. Frederick Jones the master having this day resigned his position after nearly twenty years service. After a few words from the master the boys gave a round of hearty cheers for their late and future masters.

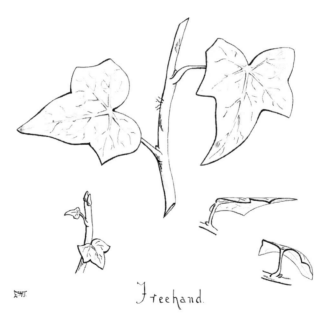

Freehand.

Sketch by Ernest Alexander Jones

Mr. Frederick Thomas Jones with some of the schoolchildren - date unknown.

FREDERICK THOMAS JONES
1891-1896

Mar. 25   Frederick Thomas Jones late an Assistant in the Higher Grade School, York Place, Brighton, commenced duties today.

Mar. 31   Examined the whole school in the 3 Rs...Unseen passages for dictation were given. The reading generally is not loud enough and the pronunciation is weak...

Apr. 1   Took the Second and Third Standards in Geography and Grammar. The children were able to distinguish the Parts of Speech but are weak in definitions...Gave a little extra time to Musical Drill today.

Apr. 8   Found out that R...had been playing truant. Mrs. R. called asking the master to punish him severely as she was unable to manage him. He received four stripes upon the hand. The village fair was held to-day.

Apr. 27   ...The schools were ordered to be thoroughly cleaned the walls to be brushed and the floors scrubbed...

May 4   ...During the afternoon the children were placed in the order in which they would be examined on the morrow by Her Majestys Inspector. The following pieces will be taken for Recitation subject to the approval of Her Majesty's Inspector.

Standard I	The Beggar Man	
Standard II	The Well of St. Keyne	Southey
Standard III	The Well of St. Keyne and	
	The Pet Lamb	Wordsworth
Standards IV, V, VI, VII	Extract from King Henry IV	

May 12   The drawing for the standards has now commenced. Special standards will be arranged as abilities in Standard work is no criterion as to art. The children chose their captains for cricket and stool ball. Frank Thatcher being chosen "Captain" of Cricket and "Alice Burton" of Stoolball.

May 29   Dr. Fussell, Medical Officer of Health visited the Schools and inspected the Girls offices. The children are particularly free from illness and the parish is free from any general sickness. Dr. Fussell remarked that the children were very clean and tidy. He visited at the time when the children were going out for recreation...

June 4   The Rev. Collett visited the schools during the morning. He saw the children perform their musical drill during the time for recreation. The Revd. Gentleman who is a manager of large schools complimented the children on the excellent way in which they performed it. During the recitation lessons the children are required to repeat it simultaneously, the master acting as a pattern. This gives great confidence to the weakest ones...

June 8   ...It is reported that measles have broken out in the village. This epidemic has been very severe in neighbouring parishes and the schools have been closed.

June 9   …Special attention was again paid this morning to writing and formation of figures. Vere Fosters bold writing is being introduced and the classes have received much practice in writing words without taking the pen from the letter. Shewed the best examples to the class, viz: those of Burt; Hunnisett; Saunders; Street.

June 19   Captain Clements visited the school and gave the boys a very strong cricket ball. The stock ordered for the school has just been received from the National Society. Each child in the school with be provided with an Exercise Book. The weather during the past week has been excessively hot - the school thermometer registering over 70 during 3 days…

July 25   No school was held in the morning. Terrific thunderstorms occurred during the morning. The lightning was very severe. The race stand at Lewes 8 miles distant was struck and partly burnt down…

July 29   No school to-day owing to the annual treat. The children assembled at 2 o'clock and after parading the village went to the Rectory. The weather was most unpropitious as rain fell in torrents during the afternoon. Three of the Managers, Captain Clements, Revd. H. Harbord and Captain Bryan attended and tried to make the day as enjoyable as possible. It was necessary, however, to terminate early…

Oct. 5   The school was opened after a vacation of 5 weeks the latter week having been given in consequence of a late hop-picking. 85 attended. The managers having accepted the Free Education Act no school fees will be paid.

Oct. 9   …Punctuality has very much improved a very few children coming in after prayer time. Several children attend from a distance of over two miles and are almost without exception punctual.

Oct. 22   There has been almost continual rain during the last four days and on Monday and Thursday the weather was most boisterous. Only 59 attended on Monday morning and 53 on Thursday morning. Although Wednesday was rough 103 and 100 attended. Captain Clements and Revd. H. Harbord visited several times, the former gentleman bringing a football for the boys game. The Revd. H. Harbord has kindly given a field rent free. The children have been well provided with materials for games, through the generosity of these two gentlemen. K. E. a girl from Framfield School has been admitted aged twelve and a half years. She made 16 mistakes in a piece of dictation which was written correctly by several children. She failed to work Standard II sum correctly.

Oct. 30   … The football club has been organised and Samuel Trill and Frank Thatcher were chosen as Captain and Vice captain…A box of material for the school arrived during the week, chiefly drawing and writing stock. A new blackboard for scale drawing has been bought…

Dec. 15   Examined in Division IV in Scale Drawing this afternoon. Most of the examples were creditably done. Attention will be paid to finish of drawings. The master, having spoken to Captain Clements about the insufficiency of the desk accommodation, this gentleman promised to procure some at once, having placed the subject on the agenda at the last Managers meeting.

1892

Jan. 4   …Several children are absent owing to the influenza epidemic. A penny bank was started to-day in connection with the schools. The trustees are Captain Clements, Revd. H. Harbord, J. Rickett, Esq. and the Master. There were 31 depositors.

Jan. 11   73 and 79 present respectively. The low attendance is due to snow, the ground being covered to a depth of nearly six inches. Mrs. Harbord visited the school during the dinner hour and gave all the children who remained for dinner a cup of hot cocoa.

Jan. 20   Through the kindness of several ladies soup dinners are provided for the children at the nominal charge of one halfpenny. These are much appreciated and 100 children partook of the 1st dinner of this year. Mrs. Harbord, Miss Clements, Mrs. Bryan and Miss Collett and the master attend to the dinner.

Jan. 25   J. Ricketts, Esq. died yesterday from an illness following an attack of influenza. The deceased gentleman was a manager of these school and an ardent supporter. His death will be mourned by all. A child named Bennett three years of age has died of diphtheria, the brother and sisters will consequently be kept at home until a doctor certifies that it will be safe to admit them.

Jan. 29   The master sent a letter from the teachers and children to Mrs. Rickett expressing sympathy with the family in their sad bereavement. A very nice wreath was also sent nearly every child subscribing to buy the requisite white flowers

Feb. 2   … The number of depositors in the penny bank at present is 51 and the deposits for last week reach 11/-…

Feb. 29   Admitted two children from Whitesmith, G. and E. N. They have been attending a dame school and are in a very backward condition. Their reading is without the slightest expression and the formation of the letters in their writing is deplorable…

Mar. 7   A quantity of stock for school use arrived to-day consisting of writing material stock for drawing examination and a supply of new books. The amount deposited weekly in the penny bank averages about 9/-. The amount would undoubtedly be much larger but many of the older scholars make deposits directly into the Post Office Bank.

Mar. 11   …Edith Carley is absent from illness. She is suffering from pleurisy and congestion of the lung… Owing to the low temperature extra time has been given to musical drill. The exercises are well done, the children taking much pain. The weakest class of the school is the 6th standard. The children forming this are considerably below the average in intellect and although extra attention is paid to them their work is oftentimes very disappointing. Several lessons on the Metric System have been given during the week.

Mar. 19   The Master received a paper from the East Sussex County Council Instruction Committee stating they were considering a scheme, for the establishment of Exhibitions to enable teachers at present engaged in public Elementary Schools within the Administrative County to attend courses of Lectures or Classes for

Technical and Manual Instruction to be held on Saturday at convenient centres (yet to be determined) during the months of May, June and July 1892.

Apr. 8   On Enquiry for absentees the master finds that several children stop away from school in order to pick flowers for which they receive a few pence at a florists. During the week the children were photographed.

Apr. 18   …The master received notice that one of the family of Hunt were suffering from measles. This epidemic has been about the parish for nearly a year.

May 6   Government Inspection: Recitation for 1893: Standards IV, V, VI, VII, The trial Scene from Merchant of Venice. Standards II and III King Bruce of Scotland. Standard I The Beggar Man.

May 19   The Lord Bishop of the Diocese visited the schools in the morning and stayed a long time. He seemed highly pleased with the large number of children who attended the school who had passed the Exemption Standard. His Lordship remarked that "they were as clean a lot of children as he had ever seen." Some musical drill also highly pleased his lordship. Remarking that the school seemed very popular the master explained that it was mainly owing to the great personal interest taken in the schools by Captain Clements and Revd. H. Harbord. The Schools were closed in the afternoon as a Confirmation service was being held in the Church.

May 23   A girl, E. H., was brought to school this morning. She comes from Sand Hill and is 10 years of age. The master on examining her found that she could not point out a letter O in a reading book and she knew absolutely nothing of writing and arithmetic. As the easiest work of this school is far too difficult for her, she has been transferred to the Infant School.

June 28   The girl J. was admitted. She is in a deplorable condition and will with difficulty reach Standard I by next year. Edith Carley was readmitted yesterday. She has suffered a very dangerous and complicated illness and for some time her life was despaired of…

July 1   Haymaking is now general but the attendance is fairly good the numbers having been over 120 all the week - the highest average for several years…During the last two months the geography of Scotland has been covered by the Upper division…The needlework garments to be made and exhibited at the Flower Show have not yet been commenced as no material has yet been supplied. These garments are made according to the government requirements for examination in that subject. This delay is seriously handicapping Miss Wenham the sewing mistress.

July 8   …In order to supply an ample quantity of unseen reading the "School Newspaper" is being taken.

July 22   F. T. has been absent for five weeks, she has been for a holiday. This is one of many examples which show to what extent the parents of some children study the master's and childrens' interest. The children of W. B. have been kept at home rook tending on their father's farm… The boy G. recently admitted to these schools will be quite unable to reach Standard I by the next examination as he cannot read monosyllables and knows nothing of writing and arithmetic.

July 26.   …A girl A. B. was brought to the school. She is an imbecile and although qualified by age to enter the big school she was sent to the Infants Department as she has no ability to learn… The prizes to be given at the coming treat were bought this week. The treat has been postponed owing to the dangerous illness of the Rector's mother.

Aug. 22   The attendance is now very bad. An enquiry into the cause of absence shows that 15 are harvesting, 9 employed in domestic duties, 5 sick and 1 employed at a florists. G. E., H. R. and R. C. have been reported so often that they seem to treat these warnings with contempt.

Aug. 25.   …The school will be closed till Monday as the village exhibition of flowers and vegetables will be held in the schoolroom tomorrow…

Oct. 7   ….The attendance officer has not yet called. Captain Clements the correspondent of the Managers is much more use in compelling the children to attend regularly than the attendance officer who calls at most once a fortnight. Captain Clements walks down to the school nearly every day and invariably asks a child why it is absent from school if he meets one in the village…

Oct. 14   … The weather has been much colder this week and consequently fires have been used…

Oct. 21   …The Upper Division have now learnt three songs and a part of each lesson is devoted to voice training…The Master examines each class in the three Rs. weekly and the results are recorded in an examination register.

Oct. 25   …Captain Clements called yesterday and arranged for the lighting of the school fires…

Oct. 27   …Fires are now lit daily.

Nov. 23   … J. B. sent home at 10 to get a collar. Three others warned.

Nov. 25   …The master told G. that unless he wore a collar and came cleaner he would have to sit by himself. Mrs. G. called stating that a scarf was worn because he suffered from bronchitis. She was asked to put a collar over the scarf. The H's were warned about collars.

Nov. 28   The H's and G's were provided with clean collars this morning…The Master has long desired to establish a Museum in the School. With this object in view, and also in order to provide better cupboard accommodation he consulted the Managers, with the result that a new cupboard having cases on the top, to hold museum specimens, will be provided. Mr. F. Jones, late Master, and a present Manager, has kindly offered to lend several interesting specimens…

Nov. 29.   Percy Hutson a scholar in the 6th Standard has received a Certificate from the office of the School Newspapers "highly commended" for Excellence in Writing.

Dec. 9   …Held a Drawing Examination on Tuesday, the results being with few exceptions, satisfactory…

Dec. 16.   Specimens for the School Museum have arrived during the week from some of the leading manufacturers…

1893

Jan. 6   …During the week Captain Clements has given an order for a new cupboard to be made. The top of this will be made to hold Museum Specimens - the whole being 14ft. long…

Feb. 3   Whooping cough which has been prevalent in our neighbouring villages has now entered our parish, appearing at Halland and Hawkhurst Common.

Feb. 13   … The boys' offices require attention and will be seen to immediately…

Mar. 1.   It is quite impossible to hold school this morning as rain has been descending in torrents and the few children who came were very wet. These were sent back by a Manager's directions.

Mar. 6   The new cupboards and museum are being put up. The Time Table will not be strictly kept in order to permit of the lessons being arranged so that the carpenters shall not interfere.

Mar. 29   The "Artists" Rifle Volunteers will lunch in the village. This is the cause of several absentees…

Apr. 11.   …The Master resumed his duties after a weeks absence through illness. The School has been conducted by Miss Wenham in a most satisfactory manner. Her discipline has been excellent… The following have received certificates from the offices of the School Newspaper, being Highly Commended for Excellence in Writing - Ernest Bellingham, Ernest Funnell, Percy Hutson and George Guy.

Apr. 28   …The Editor of the School Newspaper wrote saying that the number of Competitors in the recent Writing Competition was over 500. This school received 4 certificates out of 6 entered.

June 5   …Mrs. Harbord called and brought two models - a Patagonian man and woman for the school Museum.

June 9   The Master spoke to Captain Clements concerning the seats of the girls offices. C. C. stated that considerable alterations were contemplated…

The alterations to the offices mentioned in the above extract were those recommended at the last inspection by H.M. Inspector when he stated that "the Offices do not satisfy the requirements of Form 46 in respect of lighting and seat accommodation." The Managers were very prompt in carrying out any necessary alterations and repair work to the school and they always employed local labour, the firms of Halls and Trills being in competition with each other.

June 16   The School stock arrived this week. There are still a few cases of bad throats about. The attendance for the week has been low, partly owing to the Hay-making. This should not cause much absence however, as the crop is the smallest ever known. The Master examined the voices of all new comers this week including thirty raised from the Infant School. The Thermometer has often been above Summer heat during the week.

June 23   The rain descended in torrents until after the

commencement of school hours. The children attend very punctually now in order to obtain a red mark. As a consequence, those who ventured, were saturated, and Dr. Holman, one of the Managers, ordered them to be sent home…

June 30   …The Master punished F. P., H. C. and G. H. for interfering with cows. The misconduct of F. P. having been brought before the Correspondent he orders that this boy be not admitted to the Infant School until the Managers decide at the next Quarterly Meeting in August what is to be done with him.

July 28   The Managers at their meeting held this day had the case of F. P. under consideration. They regret extremely any child attending their school should have so misconducted himself. They trust however his not having been allowed to attend school for the last month will be a sufficient punishment and warning, and for the future he will be honest and truthful. Miss Wagon can readmit him on Tuesday next the 8th inst.

July 6   No school held to-day - a holiday being given in honour of the Royal Wedding of the Duke of York and Princess Mary of Teck. Captain Clements, whose efforts are untiring in promoting the welfare of the scholars entertained all the children (249) at Belmont where he had provided a round of amusements.

July 12.   …The new subject History is very good and the children enjoy the lessons.

Nov. 10   … Percy Turner a son of the blacksmith has died from diphtheria. A child has also died in the neighbouring parish of Ringmer from the same cause. The Ringmer schools are closed owing to a case at the school house…

Dec. 1   …The alterations connected with the offices are complete, and a pavement has been made to the girls' offices.

1894

Jan. 1   School commenced. The Holdings at Halland are absent owing to scarlatina. A severe frost has set in just now.

Jan. 5   It is impossible to open school this morning owing to a heavy snow storm. 23 degrees of frost are registered at 9 o'clock.

Jan. 8   Owing to the depth of snow it is still impossible to open school as traffic is almost blocked.

Jan. 9   Soup Dinners commenced to-day and will be given on Tuesdays and Fridays. Another girl has failed with Scarlet Fever.

Jan. 12   Jabez Hall was sent home this morning as he appeared to be sickening for some complaint.

Mar. 2   …Special attention has been given lately to the meanings of words and phrases in all the upper standards. The School Newspaper is used for unseen reading. B. Rogers presented a nice collection of butterflies to the Museum.

Mar. 5   The Quarterly Examination Reports which were suggested by the Master have proved a great boon to the school. A copy of one of these has been published in "The Teachers Aid".

Among other marks, one is awarded for Cleanliness. The Master inspected the school this morning with a view to recording any cases of unclean boots, untidy heads, want of collars. 115 were present and the following are the results for whole school: Unclean Boots 4; Untidy Heads 2; Collars missing None. In the case of the above their Quarterly Mark will be lowered.

Mr. Jones had started the quarterly reports in an attempt to stimulate the interest of the pupils and their parents in the school work. School attendance by this time had become compulsory.

Apr. 6   On inspecting the girls offices this morning the master found them working improperly. They will be attended to this evening.

Apr. 25   A hurricane was raging this morning at the time the children were coming to school. Those who did venture were wet through. By Captain Clements' orders these were sent home and it was consequently impossible to open school. The Master bought two cane handled Cricket Bats and two Stoolball bats for the two Clubs out of subscriptions given by friends of the parish. Charles Bennett and Lily Trill were elected by the children as captains of the Cricket and Stoolball Clubs respectively. During the last two seasons every game played with neighbouring parishes has been won.

June 19   A little boy, Walter Kemp, was brought to the Master during the dinner hour, having eaten some poisonous berries from the hedge. The master gave him an emetic immediately and took him to the doctor, who administered another.

June 22   The Master found one of the Boys' Offices in a bad condition. It will be altered as soon as possible…

June 25   A. A. has been absent 27 times out of the last 43 times the school has been opened. Captain Clements sent word to Mrs. A. that unless he was more regular in future she would have to attend before a bench of magistrats at Uckfield…

July 6   The last fortnight has been exceptionally hot, the school thermometer registering over 70 and to-day 78. The attendance is better, though still too low. Captain Clements and Rev. H. Harbord called often. On Monday morning the master sent home G. C., a little boy who had very bad eruptions on the face. F. G. is away from the same cause. On Thursday the Master prepared a list of Prizes to be given to the Children…

July 16   …During this Quarter special attention has been given to voice training in singing and to Physical Exercises. On Saturday the members of the School Cricket Club played a match at Uckfield against an Uckfield XI. The Rev. H. Harbord very kindly conveyed them. This gentleman has contributed very largely to the success of the Recreation Club having provided a field for the Club both for Cricket and Football.

July 20   …A half holiday was given on Wednesday as Manley's Circus gave a performance in the Village. Nearly all the children attended the afternoons entertainment.

Oct. 31   Mrs. Maples has very kindly given a number of games to amuse the scholars during the dinner hours of wet days. The master has also given a few.

Nov. 5   Double Sessions are being held this morning, to enable those children who live a long distance from the school to reach home before fireworks are set off.

Nov. 9   …George Starnes has been absent suffering from Rheumatism. This lad never enjoys good health…

Nov. 16   The Attendance has suffered greatly this week owing to inclement weather. Monday, Wednesday and Thursday were excessively wet and heavy floods have occurred in the neighbourhood. On Friday no less than eight boys were absent cover-beating…Wand and Military Drill has been taken since the holidays…

Nov. 30   … One of the Girls Offices work improperly. It will receive immediate attention.

Dec. 17   The School was used to-day as a Polling Station. The election is held under the new Local Government Act.

1895

Jan. 11   The weather has been unfavourable to attendance. A great deal of sickness continues… The Master has warned the children about venturing on deep ponds during the prevailing frost.

Feb. 1   …Snow storms have prevailed all the week. Mr. Norman and Mr. Holmes driving their children home on two occasions. The Roads are covered with snow and the cold is intense. Mrs. Harbord has very kindly sent coffee for those who took dinner at school…

Feb. 4   Through the instrumentality of Rev. H. Harbord and Captain Clements soup will be provided during the cold weather.

Feb. 8   Soup dinners commenced on Tuesday. An excellent dinner is provided for a halfpenny. Children of parents unemployed receive a free dinner. The weather is most severe, one gentleman driving about in a sledge. The thermometer has been below zero on several occasions. There are many cases of influenza in the village and many scholars are unwell…

Feb. 15   Over 120 children partook of the soup dinner this morning. Mrs. Harbord very kindly fills all basins which are distributed by Captain Clements, Rev. H. Harbord and several ladies. To-day commences the fourth week of the great frost.

Feb. 22   Owing to the excessive frost the boys offices are frozen and do not work. A thaw has just commenced…

Feb. 25.   A snow storm was prevailing at 9 this morning, the attendance falling to 74 and 85 in the morning and afternoon respectively.

Mar. 22   …The Earl of Chichester sent a case of oranges (420) to be distributed among the scholars.

Apr. 19   …Several children stop away in order to pick flowers which are sold by a professional gardener…

Apr. 25   No school opened this morning in consequence of heavy thunder showers. Several children who ventured to attend school were compelled to return. Miss Wenham was obliged to go home again.

May 3   …Harold Rich, top boy of the last Quarterly Examination in standard V is lying in Brighton Hospital with a diseased hip. He will probably be there for several weeks.

May 24   …Herbert Hemsley who was presented in Standard V on the 6th inst. died of meningitis on Wednesday Evening…

May 27   Herbert Hemsley will be buried this afternoon at 4.30. In order to allow a large number of children to attend the funeral the Managers gave orders for School to commence at 1.30, and close at 3.35. Registers closed punctually at 1.30.

Death in Victorian times was not a subject considered taboo for small children; they nearly always participated in the funerals at the Church, either by attending the service or contributing to the flowers or wreaths.

The Inspector's report on the Infants School on June 10th states that the teaching is good, but more care is needed in the formation of letters in handwriting, and he recommends that it would be wise to continue with the use of slates ruled with three lines for the babies class and a word building frame with loose letters for the two lower classes. The word building frame was ordered and duly arrived in the middle of July.

Aug. 12   The school treat took place on Friday in favourable weather being the only day for a long time during which no rain has fallen.

Oct. 21   …Mrs. Maples presented the School with a rocking horse.

Dec. 6   … A new chimney is being built.

Dec. 11   Two men are working in school to-day making a new fire place. As this will cause inconvenience the Time Table will be altered.

Dec. 13   …The Master consulted Captain Clements about the unsatisfactory manner in which the New Girls Offices work…

Dec. 19   …A workman is putting in the fireplace to-day.

Dec. 20   Mr. Hall found out the cause of the obstruction in the girls offices to-day. These have worked indifferently ever since they were built. Three large pieces of brick were found in the main pipe and have evidently been there since the construction of the offices…Many children are suffering from severe coughs and colds. Some of the bigger girls have helped the Infant Mistress occasionally as the Pupil Teachers are sitting for Queens Scholarship Examination.

1896

Jan. 15   A performance of the opera "Iolanthe" will be given by an amateur company tomorrow. This necessitates a great deal of preparation, consequently the Managers have directed double sessions to be held to-day. The Registers will be closed at 9 and 11. Recreation 10.30 and 12. Part of the proceeds will be given to the fund for mending the school yard.

Jan. 24   Captain Clements sent some oranges for the scholars. By a strange coincidence the Earl of Chichester ordered some on the same day…

Feb. 6   A Quarterly [examination] should commence this morning but the Master postponed it as he is very unwell. In the afternoon the Master had to give up and by Captain Clements instruction remained indoors. Miss Wenham was placed in charge.

Feb. 7   Mr. Jones is still very unwell and unable to come into the School. Everything has gone on satisfactorily during his absence…

Mar. 20   The family of S. from Blackboys have been continually warned about the filthy state of the childrens' heads. They have been turned away once but on promising to come clean have been allowed to attend. As further complaints are made the Managers have expelled them.

Apr. 2   The school broke up for the following day and Easter Monday. The average has fallen considerably being only 106. This is due to the large number of children who have left. M. H. is still absent. The Master sent the Attendance Officer to enquire as to her health and Mrs. H. says she is still suffering from neuralgia. She has been absent eight months. The walls were swept down on Wednesday Evening.

On the 13th April Capt. Clements noted that Mr. Jones was unable to be in School because of a severe cold and congestion on his left lung, and on the 17th April Mr. H. C. Holman, the medical attendant recommended that school be closed because of Mr. Jones' illness. School was reopened under the charge of Mr. Care on the 27th April, but in the morning of 29th April Mr. F. T. Jones died. The School was closed again on that day and Mr. Care left for Aldershot on the 1st May. During Mr. Jones' illness Miss Wagon, head teacher of the Infants, gave permission for Cecilia Cane, her Assistant Mistress, to give assistance to Miss Wenham in the Mixed School.

On the 5th May James Wilkins took charge of the school, but unfortunately the poor man lasted for a total of six days when he was asked to leave as the Managers felt the "tone and discipline of the School were likely to decline" while under his charge. The school was reopened on the 1st June 1896 under the temporary charge of Mr. R. White, who left shortly afterwards, when Miss Wenham, the first Assistant Mistress took charge until the arrival of Mr. Ernest Alexander Jones, the brother of the late Head Master.

The Inspector's report records "I wish to express my sense of the great loss which this School has experienced in the death of the late able and active Master, Mr. Jones… The thoroughly good tone and the real efficiency were the reflection of his character. These were maintained to the last. That there has been but little falling off since the beginning of his illness is, I consider mainly due to the senior Assistant, Miss Wenham."

July 20   The School Treat took place on Friday 17th inst. when over some 200 children were present. Cecilia Cane was presented on said occasion with a travelling trunk and umbrella from the Managers, Gentry, Teachers and Children."…On the 8th September 1896 Miss Cane joined the Brighton Training College.

Aug. 10   Mr. E. A. Jones took charge of the School this morning as Head Master.

Oct. 16   …Mrs. Maples presented pair of shark fins to the School Museum.

Oct. 28   Her Majesty Inspector approved of the pieces selected for recitation, viz. VI. I. Rain in Summer (Longfellow). Div II The Combat from Lady of the Lake. The following subjects for Object Lessons were also shown.

<u>Animal Life</u>: The Dog, Earthworm, A Bird (covering wings, beak, feet, motion, nest, eggs), Beaks of Birds and their uses, Feet of Birds and uses. Human teeth.

<u>Vegetable Kingdom</u>: Leaves, Roots, Stems, Seeds, Parts of a Flower, The Potato.

<u>Mineral Kingdom</u>: Minerals, A mine, Slate, Gold, Coal.

<u>On Science of Common Things</u>, A Pump, Candles, Thermometer, Compass, Petroleum, A Sponge, Things that Stretch, Forms of water, Mortar and Cement, Rain Snow.

Dec. 18   …Received two lamps for use in School today.

Dec. 22   …On Wednesday morning Rev. G. S. and Mrs. Wilson came into see the little ones at tambourine drill, awarding the children at the same with sweets…School provided with some good lamps, which were used for the first time this week.

1897

Jan. 6   Admitted the child E. S. on the 5th inst. recently from Chiddingly, who is in a very backward condition. The children resented his appearance among them at first, owing to the condition he was in; but as that improved the shrinking from him decreased.

Jan. 22   Captain Clements J.P., the Misses Clements and Miss E. Holman visited on Tuesday afternoon, when Miss Clements gave about 60 of the little ones oranges. Mrs. Clements sent down from Belmont a number of bon-bons…A new supply of stock received this day, the babies taking for the first time setting the table for tea.

Apr. 14   Very wet day. Some 44 + 1 children present, the three little Funnells coming over three miles.

May 21   …Desks for the Gallery arrived on Wednesday morning…

May 28   …The mistress, by Captain Clements wish, used a quantity of Jeyes Disinfectant about the room as Scarlet Fever has broken out in a neighbouring parish. The desks on the gallery used for the first time on Monday morning…

The Inspector's report on the 3rd July 1897 states "…The addition of desks to the baby-room gallery, which the Managers purpose to make, will be a great help to the instruction. He also comments that the school has "recovered from a temporary depression and now is in a very efficient condition again. The work is thorough and all classes are interested in it. I am glad to hear that a new Class Room is to be built."

July 12   Work on the new classroom commenced to-day…

Aug. 10   Mrs. Saunders of Brighton gave an interesting lecture on Temperance to the Upper division at 12 o'clock this morning…

Oct. 5   …Owing to the staff being less and the new class room being soon in use the Time table will be altered to suit these changes. Admitted 3 of the family of Head from Blk-Boys.

Oct. 29   … Captain Clements, J.P. and the Rector visited several times together to make arrangements about a programme of drill, etc. for the opening Ceremony of the New Victoria Classroom; when the children it is decided are to go through the Fan, Bell and Tambourine Drills, to Recite and Sing some Action Songs, this is to take place on the 12th November. Miss A. Clements came down and photographed the children and teachers on Friday morning…

Nov. 11   …Closed on Thursday afternoon for the opening of Victoria Class room on Friday.

On Friday last the new Class Room at the Mixed School was opened. Forty two children of this School attended. It was a real pleasure to see how well the little ones did their Drills, and the interest they took in the different performances. Much credit is due to Miss Wagon and her Assistants, the afternoon was thoroughly enjoyable…

Nov. 12   Whole day's holiday given, the new class room being opened and the scholars of the mixed and Infant Departmts. entertained a large company of parents and subscribers with Drills, Recitations and Singing. Every child received a bun and an apple on the occasion.

Nov. 19   …The school has been closed soon after 4 o'clock once or twice this week owing to the light. The girl, Grace Russell is absent having been taken to Brighton Hospital…This week Ruth Turner died on Wednesday morning from an internal complaint, the little ones on Friday brought a splendid lot of flowers for a floral tribute…

1898

Jan. 17   A new Blk-bd has been fixed to the wall in the "Victoria Class Room" a great improvement.

Feb. 8   Head-master wrote to all absentees and to the parents of those chn: who have been sick, urging them to endeavour by the regular attendance of their chn: now, to make up for lost time: received many letters plainly showing that the parents are not to blame, but the cause is unavoidable…

Feb. 18   … There is a marked improvement in the babies work since Phoebe Holmes has been in the Class room. Phoebe Holmes herself has shown a great change in her teaching lately, on that account she has been put into the classroom to eventually take charge of the Lower Classes.

Apr. 15   …In order to create a new life in their Colonial Geography a competition (Puzzle Pictures) has been established and is very popular with the children.

May 11   The school closed tonight for Thrs: and Frid: the occasion being the wedding of Miss Clements the daughter of Capt. Clements, J.P. Manager and Correspondent of the Schools.

May 25   … Capt. Clements informed Master that he will give the whole of the children present in the school, a treat on Tues: after Whit: week - the occasion being wedding of his eldest daughter…

June 17   Children have been taught Schumann's "Spring Song" in Upper Div: Mrs. H. Harbord has kindly given about 2 gallons of milk to the dinner children (daily) for a few weeks.

July 20   At a "Show" open to the villages of Mayfield, Heathfield, Cross-in-Hand, Waldron and East Hoathly held this date. Scholars from these schools were most successful taken "firsts" for needlework in every class entered. Mary Brown (First Class). Phoebe Holmes (First Class). P.T.'s. Infants Emma Hunt (First Class). Rose Finch (Special) Alice Cosham (First Class) Ida Ansell (First Class) Ethel Hunt (Second Class, i.e. Five 1st prizes, two 2nd prizes, 1 special)

Aug. 10   School closed for Flower Show whole day - the following boys took drawing prizes - Wm. Holmes, G. Bennett, vii, R. Berry, G. Carey, vi, A. Funnell, T. Cottingham, V. F. Evenden, W. Cornwall, iv. J. Funnell and L. Holloway iii. Map Drawing - A. Funnell and C. Evenden. Writing and Needlework prizes were many in number.

This Flower Show took place at Barham House, the home of the Squire, J. C. Rickett, and the infants were awarded six shillings for Kindergarten prizes by Captain and Mrs. Clements, and the babies had sweets from Mrs. Harbord for their work.

Aug. 11   J. C. Rickett, M.P. (For Scarborough) and Company visited the school during morning attendance and complimented the children on the work exhibited at the Flower Show…

Aug. 19.   The attendance is very bad indeed owing to petty sicknesses, a little harvest, and occasional outings. This week has been completely cut up. Tuesday a whole day's holiday was given owing to "Band of Hope" Chn's outing. Thrs: afternoon Wesleyan Treat for Sunday School Chn: The excessive hot weather makes work very difficult for children, it being impossible to keep the rooms cool. Rev. J. Brack present during Script. lessons Wed: and Frid: Capt. Clements visited several times during week. Charles H. Bennett P.T. 4th year succeeded in being placed in 1st Class (Religious Subjects Chichester Dio: Assoc:) and being top boy receives exhibition of £5 and book prizes 10/-.

Oct. 3   School began to-day after five weeks holiday…

1899

Jan 9   All the chn. attending these schools were presented with a new sixpence and a bottle of sweets by J. C. Rickett, Esq., M.P. on the occasions of the master's marriage with Miss Gifkins. Capt. Clements giving away the gifts. Rev. H. Harbord also present.

Miss Alice Gifkins had been a pupil at East Hoathly School, and for a time was also a pupil teacher. She was the daughter of Alfred Gifkins who lived at Gale Cottage and he was the head gardener to Joseph Rickett at Barham.

Mar. 3   …Captain Clements brought skipping ropes and a number of balls for the little ones.

Mar. 20   …10 new desks were placed in the main room today. They are "Hallamshire" and measure 70 feet…

Mar. 29   …Captain Clements visited and brought sweets and another lot of balls for the little ones…

May 31   Halfholiday given owing to the re-opening of the Church Organ special services etc.

June 12   Admitted a child of seven years, G. B., who has never attended school before, and is only doing so now by the Doctor's orders to see if he can bear it; he has therefore been placed in the lowest class.

June 23   …Captain Clements brought some tennis racquets for the little ones play. He also gave them sweets on Friday.

July 18   Attendance officer called. Girls have had a little extra time of late…for needlework preparing for Local Competition. Boys have had map drawing.

July 24   I gave notice that the School Treat would be held on Aug. 4th in the Rectory Grounds. Having had the loan of a very powerful Microscope the chn: were permitted to view several objects of interest and also those which have and do occur in their science work.

Aug. 4   The Annual National School Treat held in the Rectory Grounds. 75 Book-prizes being given in this Depart: to scholars having made over 375 attendances…

Aug. 22   Gave notice that whole day's holiday to be given on 23rd the "Flower Shows". The boys and girls having entered writing drawing and needlework pieces etc. for prizes.

Aug. 24   The work exhibited at the show was much praised especially two garments by L. Lawn and E. Hunt. A very poor school owing to Mr. Hoath commencing to pick hops. Managers decided to close schools for 5 weeks tonight as it will be general tomorrow and a long hoppicking is expected.

Oct. 11   A very poor attendance this is due to "covert-beating" I shall request my managers to endeavour to check this growing evil; as it is impossible to grumble at parents when they keep their chn: away.

Oct. 18   Received notice that the family of Booker, Mill Lane have Scarletina, the Finch (Olive and Evelyn) are away with "bad throats". Seven boys from St. V and VI are away "covert beating". Notice having been sent to the Managers on Sunday Oct. 22nd that the Medical Officer, Dr. Stott had ordered the schools to be closed for a fortnight or longer no school took place on Monday 23rd. The family of Edw. Hudson (which includes W. Hunnisett) having failed, a second fortnight was ordered. The family of Goldsmith having failed with Scarlatina the medical authority close for a 3rd fortnight - making a total of six weeks.

Dec. 4   After 6 weeks enforced closing the school reopened 100 and 101 present.

Dec. 6   A terrible wet morning and consequently a poor attendance. Impossible to see after 3.45…It is almost unnecessary to state that after 6 weeks hoppicking and then 6 weeks closing the scholars are behind. Every effort will be made, without undue pressure to pull them up to a higher standard by the end of the school year…

1900

Jan. 5   …The last lesson I allowed the upper girls the time to commence knitting 2 doz. or so helmets for the troops in S. Africa, 25 girls volunteered to make one and having been "started" in school the greater part will be finished at home. The boys I took in S. African affairs geographical chiefly.

On October 11th 1899 war had broken out between the British Empire and the Boer Republics of Transvaal and the Orange Free State and was immediately followed by Boer invasions of British territory. Peace was signed on May 31st 1902.

Jan. 8   I have this day had to punish several boys for smoking an evil chiefly caused by a "tuck shop" supplying them. I have threatened to turn out if it occurs again with Managers consent.

Feb. 15   Very wet morning indeed (only 80 attended in the morn: 84 after). Many away with colds two with pleurisy and 2 bronchitis. Several have swollen necks, similar to mumps but not pronounced to be such.

May 24   Children were given half hours play time this afternoon to impress upon their minds The Relief of Mafeking and the Queen's Birthday. vi and vii had Essays on them.

May 29   The children were shown the eclipse of the sun and the Head Master explained the cause to the different divisions today and yesterday…

June 9   Yesterday 8th was a whole holiday to celebrate the "Fall of Pretoria" the chn: were provided with tea, refreshments, and amusements. Each child also receiving a "button" of Lord Roberts.

June 11   Yesterday was intensely hot it is so to-day one or two of the chn: became overpowered with the heat…

June 25   Having kindly been lent "A Queen's Chocolate Box" returned from S. Africa I exhibited it to all the Scholars with a few remarks on the War.

July 3   Capt. Clements having lent me a "diary" from the seat of War it was read instead of the usual Reader.

July 4   Browning and Longfellow being selected poets for the year I have secured coloured photos of them with a view of framing them for the school walls.

July 6   … I had to severely punish R. E. to-day. He found a knife in the playground and hid it away in his "dinner-bag". I searched every boy's pocket and did not find it until I had searched many bags and overcoats.

July 16   I find in enquiry this morning that no less than 57 children are back to school that have had mumps this term.

July 23   …New stock including Foolscap, Blotting and Drawing and Exercise Books, New Cards and Slates etc., etc. received this morning…

Aug. 2   Notice given for a whole holiday for annual treat. Ellen Guy who for 5 years attended school without once absent will receive a special prize. 64 books prizes given.

Aug. 9   Having at various times received letters from scholars (who write fairly good "Exercise Book Letters") but who fail to do so when writing on note-paper, I have purchased note paper for the purpose of practical letter writing in Composition and English Lessons.

The following is a list of songs and recitation for the year for the Infants:

Division 1. Recitation	Division II: Recitation
1. King Charles and I.	1. Our Major
2. The naughty rabbit	2. Kitty Cottontail
3. Grandpapa's Umbrella	3. Dicky
4. The tale of a Rat	
5. The Dead Doll	

Songs:	Songs:
1. Fairyland	1. Babyland
2. Pickles	2. Raindrops
3. Cousin Tom	3. Little Mischief
4. The Japanese Fan	4. Billy's brother
5. The Jolly Postman	5. The Railway Train.

These songs, particularly the one rejoicing in the title "The Dead Doll", were in marked contrast to the entry for May 20th 1982 when the children entered a recorder festival at Uckfield and the piece they played was "The Wombling Song"!

Oct. 1   During the holidays the floors have been scrubbed and thoroughly cleansed. The offices have been whitewashed and painted…

Oct. 2   Captain Clements met with serious accident at Buxton on Saturday last.

Oct. 8   It is with the deepest regret that I have to record the death of Capt. Clements J.P. (at Buxton) who from 1864 until the last, took a most active part in the working and welfare of the scholars and teachers of this school. His death is a severe blow to us all.

Oct. 11   The school was closed today because of the funeral of Capt. Clements. The school chn: assembled in the Church as a last token of respect to the Manager that had laboured so much on their behalf.

Oct. 26   …Have received collection of Colonial Products for teaching Geography many will be added to School Museum.

Oct. 29   Have added new model for Stand II definitions in Geo: to take the place of the sand-tray and other models for a short time…

1901

Jan. 2   School reopened today. Rev. H. Harbord gave hamper of apples for all present before nine o'clock. They had a hint of this before the holiday…

Jan 8   A dreadful snow storm came on and still raging at nine o'clock this morning consequently only 54 present - this afternoon 58 present. Of this number 50% had over a mile to tramp home through the snow.

Jan. 14   Having received a letter from a parent relating to unclean children I have today collectively spoken to the chn: urging them all to look after themselves and their younger brothers and sisters. I shall have to write to a mother or two about their chn: coming with dirty heads.

Jan. 23   This being the first day after the death of our beloved Queen, the chn: of the Upper Standards had several articles read to them on the Nation's loss, etc. etc. in place of Composition as generally taken. The attendance officer called the case of B. O is still being enquired into.

Feb. 6   Attendance officer called. he will take steps with regard to

B. O. her age when admitted at Polegate corresponds with date given here. The parents refuse to provide us with place of birth pretending they do not know. Were summoned for non-attendance there.

Mar. 1   The girl B. O.'s parents were summoned for the non-attendance of this child. For 3 months she has not attended. They have simply ignored the officer - told him the girl was 13 etc. etc. The master then made inquiries from other masters as to age when admitted and found it as given here (although this date the parents say was wrong). He also discovers that in other schools it has been the same irregularity - has been prosecuted - but never fined. The Bench on this occasion again imposing an order for attendance. Mother pleading cause of absence "ill health"??

The problem of B. O. and her date of birth had been the cause of much annoyance to Mr. Jones and the matter was not finally resolved until April 1902 when the birth certificate was handed over and she was found to be 14 years old on 11th August 1902.

Mar. 15   Having received "Census Circular" I gave special lesson and essay on the subject; also one on "Royal Tour"

Apr. 11   A terribly wet morning raining in torrents only 82 present morning. The Assistant Inspector (H.M.I.) gave a surprise visit… This is the 3rd visit this year and on every occasion the visit has been made on a frightful wet day. It has been a striking object lesson showing how a country school suffers from "bad weather", and how a poor average attendance with loss of grant is the result of the year's work from a cause absolutely beyond the control of managers and teachers under existing regulations.

Apr. 19 … Plans for the new Cloak Room passed and forwarded to Commander Cochrane…

June 14… Old desks from Infants converted into suitable lengths etc. for small class-room being much firmer and cleaner than the old ones (placed there in 1864).

June 23 Miss Wenham having been unwell for some time past - the Rev. H. Harbord acting on the Dr's advice (Dr. H. Holman, Manager) granted her a fortnight's rest at the sea-side…

Oct. 1 Re-opened school to-day with a very small attendance 90 owing chiefly to a rumour that as the school was still used for Church it was not to be opened…

Oct. 2 Owing to the downpour this morning it was impossible for children to attend, many arriving wet. Miss Wenham unable to get [here] until 10.15 from same cause. One boy was drenched and went home, others were dried in the School House…

Oct. 17 School closed owing to the re-opening of Parish Church and the Dedication of New Vestry etc. to the late Capt. Clements.

1902

In 1902 the Education Act was passed and the County Council formed. Communication between the local Managers and the Education Committee would be necessary and someone had to be responsible for all the letter writing which would ensue. The position of Correspondent was therefore formed. The Rev. J. L. Brack, the Curate, was the first Correspondent, but when he left in February 1904 Mr. Frederick Jones

took over and maintained a steady and loyal service until his death in July 1931, when his son, Ernest Alexander Jones was elected.

The 1902 Act stipulated that the schools should have a body of Managers numbering six and that they should meet once a term. There are three Minute Books from these meetings, the first one dating from April 1903.

Jan. 7 Gave notice that the School to be closed on the 8th being required for afternoon performance of "Patience".

Jan. 7 Received notice from the Board of Education that the sum of £18 would be paid as Aid Grant for the purpose of maintaining salaries (£13) and (£5) for Minor improvements etc. fencing ceilings and floors…

Mar. 14 The attendance this week has dropped from 105 to 93 owing to epidemic influenza…many were absent half-days owing to father's and mother's etc. being "down" with it.

Mar. 25. Master failing with influenza the Managers (Rev. J. L. Brack, Rev. H. Harbord, Dr. H. Holman, Mr. F. Jones) decided to close schools tonight for Easter holiday…

Apr. 9 Half holiday given by Managers in honour of Dr. Holman's daughters marriage.

Apr. 11. Influenza is disappearing and we appear to be getting back to our normal state…

May 3 Average for week 130 but many will be leaving after tonight and as they obtain situations.

June 16   …School has been closed a month (1 week Whitsun holiday (see over) and 3 weeks by order of Medical Authority) Measles having been in almost every house.

Aug. 5   …A quantity of new material arrived including Rural Readers (Junior, Inter, Senior) Drawing apparatus, Free-arm Bds and Frames, etc. etc.

Aug. 8   Owing to Coronation, Flower-shows and Harvest attendance is suffering somewhat.

Aug. 14   Yesterday a day's holiday was given to mark the occasion of His Majesty's, King Edw. VII Coronation. The village being full of festivities - not finally closing until 12, result only 80 present this morning…

Aug. 18   Writing lesson taken throughout the school this morning for Competition Flower Show Prizes.

Aug. 20   Whole day's holiday given owing to annual Cottagers Flower Show and General Fete.

Aug. 21   Poor attendance of 100 owing probably to yesterday's and todays flower show and Sports at Cross in Hand. Buses running from village. This year has been remarkable for its "halfdays" for Coronation festivities etc.

Aug. 29   School closed for hoppicking 5 weeks. The Awards for C.E.T.'s Essay on Temperance very satisfactory 16 Book Prizes and 18 certificates being given.
Standard VII and VI: B. Hunt, W. Partridge, E. White, B. Evenden, T. Berry, R. Trill, E. Burchett.

Standard V: A. Hamper, M. Funnell, M. Finch, A. Cottingham, A. Bishop.
Standard IV: W. Westgate, R. Holding, A. Finch, being "Book Prize" Winners.

1903

Feb. 12   …Many still absent owing entirely to Epidemic Influenza…

Mar. 4   A new lot of material has been ordered including Exercise Books etc. Maps of the World and Europe and other necessary stock…

Mar. 13   …All new material has arrived. The outside of the school is being painted, occasionally to meet their requirements classes and lessons are slightly altered so that the men can have all the windows etc. at their disposal.

Mar. 18   Owing to many of the chn: reaching home drenched last night, only a poor school this morning and this afternoon due to a local Sunday Sch: Prize Distribution only 77 present. A wretched school to work with.

May 29   The County Surveyor visited during the holiday. The School walls have been cleaned and floors scrubbed during the interval.

June 19   An exceptionally heavy storm this morning as school chn: were on their way, only 85 present and many of these had to be "dried" by having fires lighted…

July 20   …Owing to a very heavy thunderstorm breaking over the village only 10 present during afternoon, dinner children being prevented from returning…

Aug. 20   Only 98 present out of 132 owing to Mr. Hoath having to suddenly commence hoppicking - an exceptionally early start.

Oct. 6.   …The schools have been thoroughly scrubbed and cleansed during the holidays…

The Schools were now being cleaned by a Mrs. Durrant, work which had been previously carried out by the pupil teachers and the scholars. Mrs. Durrant had put forward her suggestions for her duties and payments which were considered by the Managers. They were as follows: In the summer months 1s. 6d. for outside offices, 1s. dusting etc., 2s. 6d. sweeping out rooms etc. In the winter months 2s. 6d. extra in addition to these sums. The Managers recommended that the sum of 7s. a week for every week of the year should be paid for cleaning and flushing outside offices, dusting, sweeping out rooms etc. and washing school dusters, lighting fires when required, scrubbing out rooms at least 4 times a year.

In 1926 the Education Dept. at Lewes, decreed, after the visit of Mr. Piggott, the Assistant to the Director of Education, that all the school floors should be scrubbed at least once a month and not just during the school holidays. The Managers replied that this was a matter of finance and gave a breakdown of their expenses. They paid the sweepers for cleaning, lighting fires, disinfecting etc. (six rooms and closets) £26 5s. and paid Ranger & Son, the local shop, £4 8s. 3d. for cleaning materials - brooms, brushes, soap, Jeyes Fluid, etc. This new requirement caused a quite considerable headache for all concerned, not only financially, but also in finding someone to undertake the new duties, the existing cleaner and her colleagues not wishing to undertake the extra work, and therefore tendering their resignations. The situation dragged on unresolved until the appointment of Mrs. Butler of Vert Cottage, Whitesmith but she resigned in July 1927 and another cleaner had to be recruited.

Oct. 22   …About half past eight a perfect deluge caught the chn: on their way to school. 120 chn: presented themselves of these 35 were more or less drenched and sent home and 8 were dried by school fires. In the Infant School 57 presented themselves and 37 had to be sent home. This record is beyond any in the experience of the present Staff.

Dec. 4   H. E. Haig-Brown County Council Inspector visited these schools today…

Mr. Harold Haigh Brown was Inspector of Schools. In 1902 the County Council appointed a provisional Education Committee to consider the implication of the forthcoming Act and to prepare plans for carrying it out. The members of the committee appointed or reappointed Managers for all schools, drew up a uniform scale of salaries for teachers, divided the County into 11 School attendance districts and appointed officers to look after them, and also arranged for a survey of all the schools to be carried out.

1904

Jan. 5   School reopens today. 118 and 122 present…(School Slates 3 doz. arrived during the holidays).

Jan. 13   Owing to the wedding of Miss Clements and Mr. Bonnick the Managers gave the chn: a half holiday…

Jan. 18   Owing to the Foxhounds meeting in the village, lessons altered to allow "playtime" to be at 11 o'clock, and chn: under teachers attended.

Jan. 29   Several articles of Stock (paper, exercise pens, etc.) arrived to-day…

Apr. 22   …Final examinations to be made next week to close school year. Chn: will be sent up or kept back not so much on this examination as by the work they have shown in their respective classes from day to day.

Apr. 25   …Scripture Examination in the morning 9 to 9.45. for the Rector's prizes continues. Upper division boys photographed at their Free-arm lesson. Attendance is still high.

Apr. 28   Rector visited this morning and tested for Fire Drill the chn: were out of school in excellent order and at their lines in the playgrounds in less than one and a half minutes.

May 13   …Started Free arm in Stands 1 and 2.

May 20   …The screen to be erected during the vacation.

In April 1903 Mr. Jones had put before the Managers a scheme for alteration of the staff with a view to improving the efficiency of the School teaching. He felt it would be advisable to remove Standard I from the Infants to the Mixed School, thus reducing the staff in the Infant School to one mistress and one pupil teacher, and the Mixed Department should be run by the Headmaster with two assistant teachers and one pupil teacher. This alteration would mean that the large school room would need a screen partition of moveable folds so that the room could be used as one room or two. It would give the headmaster more control as the pupil teacher would be with the Master. Tenders were obtained from Mr. R. Hall and Mr. A. Trill, both local builders. The estimates were - Mr. Hall - £24 7s. 6d. and Mr. Trill - £23 10s.

June 1   …Screen partly finished the overhead part not being completed.

July 27   Owing to the funeral of the late Mrs. Clements the school was closed during the afternoon.

Aug. 23   Children attending Band of Hope Annual outing. There has been more than the usual number of treats etc. etc. this Autumn. Attendance suffering considerably thereby. School closed this afternoon by order of the Sanitary Authority owing to one case of Diphtheria and a few suspected cases.

Nov. 8   Rev. H. Harbord, Col. L. F. Thompson, J.P., Dr. H. Holman, Mr. P. Ranger and F. Jones (Correspt.) visited to inspect new screen…

The East Sussex County Council wished that East Hoathly School should be recognised as a one department school, abolishing the separate department for the infants. This was on the condition that the Infant

Department was placed under a trained certificated female assistant. This arrangement would upgrade the school to Grade IV and the Master's salary should be according to scale. The post of Head Mistress of the Infant School was advertised and the Managers considered employing a Miss Crocker of Brighton. Unfortunately this lady, wishing to visit her mother in Brighton weekly, felt unequal to the walk from Uckfield in time for School every Monday morning, so she withdrew her application, and a Miss K. C. Harring from Greatham, Liss, Hants was employed instead. She began her duties on the 23rd January 1905. Mrs. Jones acted as supply teacher in the interval.

H.M.I. Mr. Gardner inspected the school on the 9th October 1906 and was unhappy with the teaching and discipline in the Infant School and the Managers, after hearing Miss Harring's explanation decided she should be asked to resign her post.

Dec. 12   During the last two months the Scholars have been fortunate in winning rather more than their share of prizes in Sussex Express Competition. The following have won Composition Prizes: A. Packham, B. Walters, B. Potter, F. Kemp, M. Chapman. Map Drawing: A. Boniface. Drawing: T. Holloway.

Dec. 16   Proportion and circulating decimals taught to v and vi. School is to close on Thrs. the 22nd. Requisitions are signed and forwarded

1905

Jan. 10   School material in the shape of Foolscap and Exercise Book, New Registers and a Log Book came today.

Jan. 11   Owing to the opening ceremony of a new organ in the Chapel, School did not meet during the afternoon.

Feb. 4   …The Rev. H. Harbord presented all the chn: present on Friday morning (as well as the genuine sick at home, with an orange each…

Feb. 17   …The Attendance is still kept low by "mumps" and cases of debility (with Dr. Certs.) following influenza etc.

Feb. 27   …E. T. suffering from St. Vitus Dance will probably be absent months.

May 5   Mrs. Harbord presented all the scholars present with chocolates - the gift of a lady…The new material arrived May 2nd including new histories on "The Stuart Period" Laws of Health etc. for new year's work.

May 22   May Burfield in St. vi won the "Sussex Express" prize for General Knowledge "Answers" in Chn: Page.

May 24   Today being "Empire Day" suitable "Object Lessons" were given. The Rev. H. Harbord presented the chn: with "Sweets".

June 14   The boy Alfred Hare died on Wednesday (June 14th) under Chloroform during operation for adenoids etc.

June 16   Chn: sent wreath, and school began at 1.30 and closed 3.30 the funeral of Alfred Hare being at 4 o'clock…

June 19   The result of the examinations for Honours Certificates is very highly satisfactory when compared with the results of East Sussex in general. Altogether 282 entered and 270 were examined with the following results:

	East Sussex			E. Hoathly	
Class 1	27	10%	1	3	21%
Class 2	51	19%	2	7	50%
Class 3	73	27%	3	3	21%
Failure	119	44%		1	7%

i.e. This school had 92% passed compared with 56% in East Sussex.

July 20   Whole day holiday, annual school treat. 220 scholars in all present. Prizes given (76) for attendance and good conduct; also for First Class in Honours Certificate Exam: and for Drawing and Needlework in respective standards. The Rector also gave his "Scripture Prizes" to the winners in each standard. It was a most successful gathering, favoured by a glorious day.

Aug. 3   The Marquis of Abergavenny visited the school and expressed himself greatly pleased and further he gave the Hdmaster 50/- to buy the chn. "Buns and sweets" to bear in mind his visit.

Aug. 9   Owing to a Primrose Fete being held at Whyly in the parish it was decided by the managers to give half holiday.

Aug. 11   The Chn: (204) were each presented with a large bun and a souvenir packet of sweets. The Rector made appropriate references to the Marquis of Abergavenny (the donor) and cheers etc. were given…

Aug. 21   Notice has been forwarded that owing to hop-picking beginning on Tuesday (22nd) school closes on that date and reassembles first Monday in October.

Oct. 20   Special lessons given on "The Nelson Centenary" Pictures etc. being shown.

Oct. 31   The scheme of (voluntary) "General Knowledge" Homework, commenced 3 weeks ago is apparently very popular with the children and parents, no less than 30 worked them carefully last week.

Dec. 23   School closed for Xmas holidays (2 weeks) General Knowledge Prizes (HdMaster's awards) were given today. 7 books and small gifts to all who worked the whole of the lists. Chief winners: Reg. Turner, Nellie and Maude Chapman, Grace and Connie Ellis, Lily Boniface, G. Jones, P. Whitewood, L. Hall, B. Potter, L. Cole, E. Cane etc. HdMaster presented all present with a picture post card (coloured) of a view in Great Britain.

1906

Jan. 8   School re-opened…Mrs. Jones still in Temporary Supply.

Feb. 23   The school examined today by the Rev. W. Walsh in Religious Knowledge - registers not marked - we were the first schools to be examined by him under the "Winchester Syllabus" and received the highest mark which he awards in every division and group.

Apr. 23   Notification has been received that henceforth these Schools are known to the Education Board as the East Hoathly National School. No. 44. *[This was changed in November 1906 to East Hoathly Church of England School.]*

Apr. 25   School material received today including Literary Readers, Nelsons and Cassells "Household Management" (McDougalls) Exercise books and other stock material.

May 25   … On Thursday (24th Empire Day) the Rector, Miss Fielding, Mrs. Maples, Rev. H. M. S. Bankart, several parents and friends listened to an address to the children given by the Rector. The children sang "The Flag of Britain", "Rule Britannia" and God Save the King. The Rector presented every child with sweets. Lessons somewhat altered from timetable to admit of specially "Marking" the day.

June 26   Managers at a meeting decided to exclude I. C. owing to the filthy condition of her head.

June 28   Half holiday granted. Three of the Staff wishing to attend the Annual G.F.S. meeting at Sheffield Park.

G.F.S. was the Girls' Friendly Society, a very popular organisation for the promotion of spiritual and material welfare of its members and to promote the virtues of family life; it's aim was also to cross the divide of class differences.

July 2   The girl C. back again, an effort has certainly been made to clean the child's head.

July 20   School closed to-day for annual Prize Distribution and Treat. H. Hunt and W. Kemp won Medals…

New rules for a prize scheme by the Education Authority had come into force on January 1st 1906. 2 candidates were awarded medals and 68 awarded certificates in the Mixed Department and 10 candidates awarded certificates in the Infant Department.

July 27   …Attendance for the Quarter ending July 146.48 the highest ever yet reached in this school.

Oct. 8   Sanitary Officer (Mr. Philips) inspected schools and offices and pronounced himself quite satisfied with their clean and sanitary condition.

Oct. 20   Week's work satisfactory each teacher has weekly record books to keep posted up. Standard iii require considerable attention, otherwise they will go back.

Nov. 26   P. Wren, P. Whitewood, and S. Whitewood are notified to be down with Scarlet Fever. The Managers decided to close the school tomorrow awaiting Medical Officer's decision.

Nov. 27   Sanitary Inspector visited today and ordered the schools to remain closed until Monday Dec. 10th. The Schools have been thoroughly cleaned and disinfected. Outdoor offices treated similarly.

On November 26th three children fell ill with scarlet fever and in a letter from T. D. Phillips, Sanitary Inspector for the R.D.C. of Uckfield - Crowborough it was recommended that all the floors should be "thoroughly scrubbed with carbolic (soft) soap and water; walls, maps etc. to be dusted down, dust to be removed from window ledges, beams or other parts of the premises; desks or other furniture and woodwork to be wiped with cloths damped in disinfectants." He also recommended the school cesspools were emptied and the offices limewashed throughout. He would then have the premises disinfected with formalin. All the books used by the children with scarlet fever were to be destroyed.

Dec. 10   School re-opened after fortnights closing, there having been no fresh cases in the interval…

Dec. 12   Attendance officer succeeded in bringing along all not unwell…

1907

Jan. 7   Schools reopen today after 5 weeks closing for Scarlet Fever - coming so soon after the long hoppicking holiday it will require much hard work to pick up lost time, especially as the staff is so few.

Jan. 10   Head Master gave Magic Lantern on "The Events of the Past Year (06)" 50 slides during the last lesson.

Feb. 28   Sent home family of Peckhams on Dr. Lovell Keays advice, chicken pox.

Mar. 1   …Elsie Price 6 yrs. Grace Roberts (Anecdotes) Cyril Hall (letterwriting) won prizes in "Sussex" Express Competitions since Christmas.

Apr. 30   End of School year. Average for year 140.6. Only opened 393 times owing to outbreak of Scarlet Fever in Nov., Dec. and Jan. when closed by Sanitary Authority for 3 weeks and 4 days (38 school meetings)

June 21   …Connie Ellis and Harriett Funnell have just recently won Prizes for "Letter Writing" (Express)…

Aug. 21   Half holiday to-day owing to Local Sunday School Treats (School and Wesleyan) and Flower Show (Framfield) Attendance officer called on Family of B's also in the case of chn: employed picking up tennis balls…

Oct. 7   School reopened this morning. Inspite of rain 141 were present out of 150 on books…

Oct. 8   A very wet morning - continual downpour - only 86 present. Many wet footed, etc. Fires lighted and children dried. Meeting abandoned. Usual work went on as far as possible.

Oct. 18   Ernest Allcorn at school on Monday died on Friday (appendicitis). Rev. H. Harbord, Miss Fielding and Mrs. Maples visited. The last named two giving all the children cake for "lunch" on Tuesday.

Dec. 6   Attendance this week has been very good indeed reaching 140 again 98%. The Concert keeps the children interested and eager to be present…

Dec. 20   School closed after morning meeting for Xmas Holiday - reopening Tuesday Dec. 31st. School concert takes place tonight. School concert by general consent was a great success.

1908

Jan. 8   Owing to a heavy fall of snow and the consequent wet and almost impassable conditions of the foottracks and roads, only forty children attended and nearly all of these had to have their

Photograph taken on 25th April 1907 of the children with their free-arm drawing boards. Headmaster Mr Alec Jones

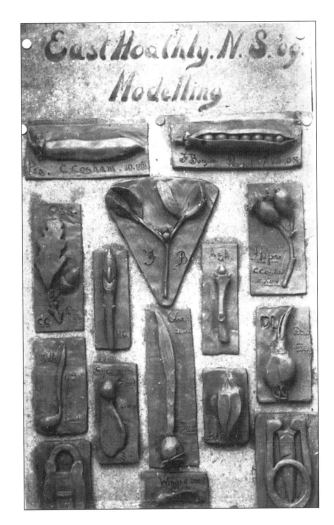

East Hoathly National Schools Modelling in 1909.
There are two models by C. Cosham – the closed pea pod and
the rosehips, and oak leaf has the initials C.C. The slightly
opened pea pod is by F. Burgess and the mistletoe in the middle
bears the initials F.B.
(If any readers know how these were done, I should love to know J.S.)

stockings and boots dried before they could take their place in the class. Registers not marked.

Feb. 7   The family of Driver absent, father accidentally killed by colt…

Feb. 14   The Managers at their meeting to-day at Head Master's request directed the offices to be cleaned out and whitewashed and the windows of schools to be cleaned.

Mar. 4   Meeting abandoned owing to snow etc. only 77 being present.

Mar. 6   Terrific rain storm prevailed this morning only 44 present…

May 22   At 3 o'clock the children sang several patriotic songs and listened to an address on the Empire given by Rev. H. Harbord, Chairman of Managers after which Miss Fielding (Local Authority's Manager) hoisted the Union Jack presented by the East Sussex Authority. Mr. P. Ranger (Parish Manager) and many friends and parents were present. Sweets were distributed and prayers and dismissal followed 4 o'clock.

 Dec. 4   Medical Inspector visited for first inspection. Infants and over 13 years of age first taken for routine inspection.

Dec. 7-8   Inspection going on. Parents took every advantage of the medical inspectors attendance, many personally consulting with him.

Dec. 10   A terrific rain storm prevailed this morning, only 30

children present in mixed and 12 in Infants, several of these very wet. Registers not marked - this is first break in them since re-opening.

1909

Mar. 3   Owing to another heavy fall of snow only 30 children present. Registers not marked…

Mar. 4   More snow, poorer attendance only 27 present.; the number of chn: on books, that have long distances to come, is very great consequently the wretched attendance.

Mar. 5   Only 74 and 70 present…By far the worst week for many months.

There had been blizzard conditions from the end of December until the middle of January when a thaw set in, but by March it was snowing again, but in calm windless conditions, so creating scenes of great beauty.

In 1908 the Managers had decided, after consulting the Head Master, that the Mixed and Infants Departments should be amalgamated, and in the Religious Knowledge Examination Report this change was noted and approved. The standard of work was high and great credit was given to Mr. Jones and all those who took part in the teaching of religious instruction.

The Managers had again approached the two local builders for painting the whole of the exterior woodwork of the Schools, Master's

House and Offices; and Mr. Hall's estimate was accepted at £11 15s. 0d. being 2s. 6d. lower than that submitted by Mr. Trill. The Master's scullery walls were also to be whitewashed. Cesspools were emptied and Mr. Hall was ordered to mend broken tiles and replace broken chimney pots

May 24   Empire Day. Children had Wednesday's lessons and public tea in playing fields.

May 28   School closed for Whitsun holiday. This year Managers granted a fortnight. Offices have been thoroughly cleaned and lime-washed seats and interiors painted.

June 14   School reassembled after recess. 167 children present out of 169.

June 18   … Lily Cottingham who has not returned since May 28th is reported suffering from whooping cough (her cousins visited her from Bognor at Whitsun-tide suffering from same).

June 21   Annie Brown reported down with whooping-cough excluded Emily Percy and Albert. The last outbreak of this complaint being so many years ago one now if not checked early will go heavily through the school.

July 23   The three candidates that sat for Minor Scholarships in May last have just received notice that each of them was successful viz. G. M. Ellis, H. Morley and A. W. Bennett.

July 26   New books added to Stock for Extension Class, viz. Nelson's "The World and its People", Pitmans "Evolutary History" and Evans "Science Readers" and Pitman's "School Dictionary" etc.

July 28   Instead of Organised Games the Head Master took the children in the Upper Group to Uckfield to see a Menagerie, returned about 7 o'clock.

Oct. 15   … At a Managers Meeting it was resolved to remove Infant's gallery at a near future date.

This was at the suggestion of Mr. Haigh Brown and agreed to on the understanding that the Education Authority provided the proper Kindergarten seats and tables.

Dec. 2   Head Master gave a "Lecture on India" illustrated by 50 coloured views shown by acetylene gas lantern after school. 170 children present.

Dec. 7   …Received 12 Bronze Medals for Cricketers, the runners up in the Hailsham and District League.

1910

Jan. 4   School reopened today, good attendance 160 present out of 167. Miss Wenham absent from her duties owing to the sudden death of her mother during the recent vacation.

Jan. 7   Headmaster gave Lantern Lecture on "The Granary of the Empire" (Canada 50 slides)…

Jan. 21   School closed owing to the room being used as a Polling Station (Eastbourne Parliamentary Division).

Jan. 28   Owing to the prevailing rain storm only about 53% of scholars present, 59 in Mixed and 19 in Infants, many of these arriving late and wet. Registers not marked. The Board of Education has notified that the Revised Accommodation of these schools is as follows, viz:

Present	Mixed	175	Revised	143	Mixed.
	Infants	93		74	Infants
	Total	268	Total	217	

The Managers at their meeting today decided to improve the entrance to children's play ground.

Mar. 16   The Scholars (42 in number) have commenced taking the St. George's Magazine

In March the Managers received a communication from Edwin Young regarding the election of Managers, delegation of their powers, appointment of teachers etc. The Managers arranged the dates of school holidays and were allowed to sell needlework and remit the amount to the Education Committee. From April 1st 1910 they had the additional power of ordering and repairing school furniture, the amount not to exceed £2 at any one time. An advance for petty cash at the rate of £1 per school could also be made to cover postages. A postage book had to be kept giving all details.

Mar. 21   Owing to the spread of measles in the school (Miss Horton, Asst. Mistress, T. A. Jones, School House, George Pankhurst, G. Roberts, L. Tuppen, A. Bennett, H. Whitewood, R. Eade and probably other families) the Authority decided to close the Schools today and until further notice.

Apr. 11   Dr. Fullerton, School Medical Officer instructed that the Schools should reopen today (wire received 7.45 Saturday 9th) Only 104 present Monday morning, probably notice of opening had not reached some…

May 6   King Edward VII died…

May 9   After morning meeting Scholars assembled in playground. The Rector read proclamation of George V and chn; sand God Save the King.

Copy of Report made by H.M.S. Inspector after visit of 8th June 1910.

<u>Schemes</u>   In addition to a satisfactory curriculum for the ordinary classes there is a distinct effort to secure independent work by the elder children, for whom suitable text books have been provided. This arrangement might be amplified and more time might be given to it.

<u>Handwork</u>   Handwork is taken throughout the School and is connected with the Nature Study and Drawing but so far it has been confined almost exclusively to the boys.

<u>Staff</u>   The Staff is sufficient, but full use is not made of it, one uncertificated teacher in the lower division has a class of 13 which is not necessitated by the educational requirements. It is also clear that, except for Mr. Jones, the head master, who is very competent, does not get the support which is reasonably to be expected.

<u>Needlework</u>   There is no fixed day for the repair of garments; this should be undertaken fortnightly, and material for the purpose should be brought by the girls from home.

<u>Physical Exercises</u> At the inspection the children were taken in Physical Exercises as one class by the Head Master, who is by far the most competent teacher in this subject, and the exercises were very thoroughly performed; but in some exercises the divisions and the sexes should be taken separately, and the staff should be trained to do their own work under the Head Teacher.

<u>General</u> The children of the upper division are doing good work, take an active and intelligent part in the subject in hand, and can use the information they possess; the lowest class is also very fairly prepared, but the two intermediate classes depend too much on their teachers, and the methods of instruction are not calculated to quicken their powers of observation; neither by practice nor by precept is there any encouragement to the children to give expression to ideas conceived in the course of a lesson.

<u>Library etc.</u> The School possesses a good supply of Literary Reading books and a library of 300 or 400 volumes, which is used in winter time by about 20 scholars.

<u>Infants' Class</u> The Infants are reticent and too dependent on the teachers who are too much inclined to do the work for them. An attempt should be made to arouse individual effort among the children, and to train them to observe and to give expression by word and hand to what they have observed. They talked freely towards the end of the lesson with H.M. Inspector…

July 15   Owing to several Sunday School Outings, Agric: Show at Eastbourne, etc. attendance has dropped this week to 93%. The new classification appears to be working well and staff are earnestly entering in the work.

Dec. 9   …Grace Saunders won Mrs. Harbord's prize for best essay on C.E.T.S. lecture.

Dec. 14   Closed School being used for Polling Station.

1911

Mar. 24   Notice received that George Pankhurst had passed Lab. Cert. Exam.

Mar. 31   … Infants have been out of doors on one or two days this week for nature and observation lessons.

The 22nd March is recorded as being extremely warm for the time of year with temperatures in the 60s, but there were blizzards and strong winds within days and then at the very end of March it all changed again with spring returning. However, by the 5th April snow reappeared.

Apr. 5   Owing to the remarkable fall of snow only 31 chn: (Mixed and Infants) present at 9.15 Registers not marked.

Apr. 13   School closed for Easter Holiday, the managers deciding to close until May 1st.

June 28   Submitted "Requisition List" to managers. Cardboard modelling material.

July 4   Attendance officer informed master this school top of District for attendance during June. 9 Scouts absent gone to Windsor (King's Rally).

July 18   No school afternoon owing to wedding of Rector's eldest son, Mr. H. C. Harbord and Miss V. M. Hornby.

July 29   (Saturday) Annual prize distribution and School Treat in Rectory Fields.

Aug. 4   Attendance very fair, progress as usual. Hot weather makes children somewhat listless and sleepy.

Oct. 2   School reopened. The schools have been varnish[ed], painted and colour-washed internally during the holidays. The gallery has been removed and the Authority grant "Dual Desks" not "Tables and Chairs" as requested by Correspondent.

Richard Hall charged £22 2s. 6d. for painting and varnishing and £4 4s. 6d. for repairing the floors. The Education Committee paid 85% of this bill. For removing the gallery, putting in sleeper wall and new joists, covering floor with new board, fixing new matchboard where necessary and varnishing the grand sum of £8 was charged.

Nov. 3   The new organisation works well. Gives scholars a much broader teaching and should tell in their general intelligence. Chief change being Tues and Thrs. when Mrs. Jones takes Infants, Miss Colebrook Lower Group; (Std. I), Miss Wenham Upper Part of Lower Division (Std. II and III) and Headmaster Upper Division (Old IV, V, VI etc.).

Nov. 20   Outbreak of Chicken-pox… Wired to Medical Officer.

Nov. 23   Mrs. Jones absent from duties nursing her daughter "Cissie" (appendicitis).

Nov. 27   No school. Headmasters little girl died at 8.30 but school had previously been stopped to secure for her perfect quiet.

Nov. 28   School reopened, poor attendance. Rains prevent many and chicken pox still spreading.

Dec. 1   No School - funeral of Head Master's little Cissie, a late scholar.

Dec. 4   Several fresh cases of chicken-pox… Mrs. Jones not yet able to return to her duties.

1912

Jan. 2   Schools reopened. Mrs. Jones back to duty.

Jan. 17   On Wednesday afternoon (play hour) the Misses Campbell-Johnstone, Harbord and Playne kindly acted the "Blue Willow" drama for the benefit of the scholars.

Jan. 22   More chicken-pox…

Jan. 26   On Tues: admitted a girl F. from Waldron district. Head had been in bad condition, nits after a fortnight's treatment apparently dead. Child residing with grandmother lately widowed.

Apr. 13   The death of Dr. H. C. Holman took place today (Sat). the deceased gentleman has been a School Manager since the schools were built in 1863.

July 10   Headmaster with 16 boys left organised games in charge of Assistant (2.45) and walked to Blackboys to play Blackboys School Cricket Team. Sch. Treat fixed for 26th inst.

July 12   Result of recent Scholarship Exam. received. T. A. Jones (11) won a Scholarship (Minor), D. Atkins (12) and K. E. M. Price reached Scholarship standard, but K. Ellis (12) did not.

July 17   Headmaster with Upper Group (2 teams, 32 chn:) walked through fields to Laughton to play cricket and Stoolball starting 2.45.

Aug. 9   Attendance remains good, school exceptionally free of sickness.

Aug. 23   School closed for 5 weeks to be reopened on Sept. 30th. Quarterly Examinations concluded. Several older girls leave tonight. T. A. Jones winner of County Scholarship (Minor) to commence at Uckfield Grammar Sc. on Sept. 10th.

Oct. 2   Instead of organized Games in the Upper Group (during Winter months) Boys will take card-board modelling and Girls Paper-flower making or Doll-dressing, etc.

Nov. 15   Lt. Colonel L. C. F. Thompson J.P. (Manager) called today and expressed the wish to present every child on the Registers with a woollen "sweater" or "jersey".

Nov. 27   R. and E. B. crawled into Sch. at 2 o.c consequently marked "absent". This family is the worst the Sch: ever had.

1913

Jan. 6   Schools reopened 137 present… Admitted family of B., very backward, one girl…aged 13 not having attended a school previously. During holidays Headmaster gave each girl a woollen jersey and boys either a cardigan, jacket or jersey, the present of Colonel L. F. C. Thompson. Children presented Colonel with a silver mounted and engraved "hunting crop".

Jan. 20   Exceptional hailstorms drenched children on their way home, result only 125 present next morning. …

Feb. 14   Attendance the highest during the school year. 144+.

Mar. 19   Registers not marked owing to the extremely rough and wet weather prevailing. 87 present. This is the only time this winter that children have been so kept away or arrived so wet, and so caused no registration.

Apr. 1   …School reopened…Classes rearranged. New work commenced.

July 11   Two candidates (N. Siggs and K. E. Price) for Minor Scholarships both reached scholarship Standard.

July 25   …Headmaster had to punish K. F. for stealing money recd. for Garden produce…

Aug. 13   Copy of Report made by H.M.I. C. Boutflower, Esq. after visit of July 25th - "A good start has been made with this School garden. It is satisfactory to learn that an additional 5 rods will be available another season which will bring the total area up to 20 rods and will enable the scope of the teaching to be broadened so as to include something beyond the cultivation of vegetables only." …

Aug. 26   Schools closed - next day being Flower Show and following that Sunday School Treats. Managers decided to close for long holiday.

Oct. 6   (Monday) School reopened after long vacation. School buildings thoroughly cleaned from roof to floor. 142 present out of 146.

Oct. 10   All the boys and girls in Mixed and Infants were measured today for cloaks and cardigans respectively, Colonel L. C. F. Thompson J.P. (Manager) wishing to give every child one before Christmas.

Nov. 17   Tchr. of infants (Lower) noticed H. Barden peeling, told Headmaster, boy having been ill and away from school, case rather suspicious. Headmaster took necessary steps to prevent (if epidemic) from spreading - probably too late.

Nov. 18   Family of Barden 5 in number absent by Doctor's orders, suspected case of Scarlet Fever.

Nov. 22   No further developments of above. By special request of Col. L. C. F. Thompson Headmaster presented every child with long cloak and hood (girls) and cardigan woollen jacket (boys). This is the third winter the Colonel has remembered the children. ...

Nov. 26   This morning - child Cyril Burton - at school on Monday (Upper Group) to be suffering from Scarlet Fever.

Dec. 1   Barden family (5) certified by Dr. Webb as able to return to school after fortnight's exclusion.

1914

Jan. 31   New shelves have been put up in the old disused lobby thereby rendering the same a very useful Store Cupboard a much reqd. boon.

Feb. 6   Attendance slightly affected by coughs and colds. School top of district again (93%)…

July 10   New goods received as per Stock Books including Oxford Readers for Std. V and III, also Literary Readers for Middle and Lower Groups and a few for Infants.

The following Report by H.M.I. C. Boutflower, Esq. was received by the Managers:- "The teaching is most earnest and thorough and very valuable work is being done. An Arithmetic test set to the top section was exceptionally well done and the care taken to secure clear and logical arrangement in the working of the sums deserves the highest praise. A particularly interesting History syllabus based on the local history of the neighbourhood is typical of the progressive character of the instruction as a whole.

Drawing is taught with very satisfactory success and the girls take the keenest interest in their needlework, and produce some remarkably good sewing.

The methods employed in the Infants Division have improved and better results are discernible here than was the case at the last visit of Inspection.

Certain points have been discussed with the Headmaster and class teachers such as the question of providing more advanced work for the best children in the top class, the desirability of taking more free Composition in the early stages and the importance of practical and observational work in the Geography of the Juniors. These will no doubt receive his careful consideration.

Gardening is taught with the same care as the rest of the School subjects. Some of the ground is very poor and would benefit by a more liberal allowance of manure. The surface of the Playground is not good for Physical Exercises." …

July 22   …T. A. Jones a minor scholarship holder from this school notified that he had gained his Intermediate. Doris Atkins also notified she had won P.T. scholarship.

Aug. 4   School reopened this morning. Average for last quarter 139.5 (War declared last night against Austria and Germany)

Aug. 14   Attendance fairly good; owing to outbreak of war Flower Shows and Fetes etc. are postponed or abandoned and consequently usual poor attendance of this month not so noticeable.

Aug. 19   …Notices relating to war matters posted up

Oct. 23   Progress and attendance continue satisfactory. Garden sales for last year £3 5s. 11d. Requisition for seeds etc. forwarded. New Register for next year's Garden Class received today.

Oct. 28   Children and staff sent £1 12s. 3d. to Princess Mary's Fund for Soldiers and Sailors (gifts Xmas).

Nov. 4   Rev. H. Harbord after 32 years as Rector and Chairman of Managers came and said "Good-bye" having retired from the "living". Children received apples and sweets…

Nov. 16   …Number of children left for work greater than in other years due to war plenty of employment offered.

Nov. 27   …Attendance down to 126 due to sores and few cases of whooping cough. Saw local doctors who said sores were "impetigo contagiouso" and have notified Authority at Lewes.

Dec. 14   J. C. sent to school sores still on hands between fingers. Headmaster sent her back home again. Owing to sickness Managers decided to close on Friday 18th for a fortnight.

Dec. 15   Owing to colds and epidemics attendance down to 95 out of 146.

Dec. 17   School closed for Christmas holiday reopen on Jan 4th much sickness due to Whooping Cough.

1915

Jan. 7   Headmaster in bed (influenza)…County Medical Authority ordered schools to close owing to increasing no. of cases of Epidemic (Whooping Cough chiefly)

Jan. 25   Reopened after closure for fortnight and a day …

Feb. 4   The school continues to suffer cruelly from epidemic. 40 absent due to whooping cough (in many cases renewed) and Impetigo in family of W. and N. The progress of class work is of course hindered.

Feb. 9   Pouring wet morning owing to colds parents are exceedingly nervous of their children, only 71 present in both departments (19 infants, 52 mixed). Registers not marked.

Feb. 12   Dr. Dunstan, Assistant Medical Officer of Health visited and examined various "special cases" and made enquiries about the outbreak of "impetigo". No troops have used these schools.

Feb. 26   … School closed 3.30 owing to 13th Manchesters using rooms for sleeping.

Mar. 1   …There are still 20 cases of whooping cough. Although many are back they cough badly.

Mar. 18   Scripture Examination usual afternoon holiday postponed until tomorrow owing to Schools being wanted to billet 225 soldiers (South Lancashire).

The Managers resolved at their meeting in May to draw the attention of the Education Committee to the low attendance due to the epidemics since October and requesting "that the headmaster's salary may not be reduced in consequence thereof."

The entry for 29th October in the Managers' Minute Books reads: "The Master brought before the Managers the New Roll of Honour, a list of gallant men who are now so nobly serving His Majesty the King on Sea and Land. This will be hung in the school to commemorate the brave actions of our parishioners and old school boys in defending their country."

1916

Nov. 3   … The little scholar Henry Hobden, who died Oct. 21st is certified to have died of "acute-anterior polyo-myolitis".

At a Managers' meeting the finances were dealt with. The Balance in the bank book and school ledger was £45 14s. 0d. No subscriptions had been paid since 1914 because of the war. Twelve years previously the subscriptions had amounted to £12 4s. 0d. The painting of the school and the inside cleaning was overdue and the Correspondent viewed "with alarm a diminishing balance." The County Council contributed to salaries, fuel and cleaning, but made no contribution to repairs, so a special effort had to be made to obtain new subscriptions. On the 23rd March 1917 a letter was distributed appealing for funds.

In November 1919 a further letter was sent. The balance now stood at £30 16s. 3d. On the 5th November 1920 it was reported to the Managers that the subscriptions amounted to £13 4s. and a further £30 was needed. Colonel Thompson donated £10.

In February 1920 a Bazaar was held to raise funds, resulting in £100 10s. By February 1921 the balance amounted to £124 13s. 6d., a much healthier situation. A cheque for £5 had also been received from Bettons Charity.

As a result of the increased finances repair work could now be carried out and estimates for painting, varnishing, distempering the interior of the schools, the repair of lavatories with two new basins, sundry repairs to the bell turret, pavement etc. were obtained. In sealed bids Hall & Sons submitted a tender of £68 10s. and Trill Bros. one for £122. Work on the Master's House was deferred.

The inside of the schools had been last decorated in 1911 when the cost was £27 10s. Previously this work had been carried out every five years without fail. The lavatory had been in use for over 50 years, and the Gardening Class made it essential to have more than two basins! The Managers also thought a cycle shed would be a good idea, if possible.

1919

Jan. 16   Rifleman, C. G. Ansell, a former Pupil Teacher of these schools at special request of Head gave stds. iii, iv, v and vi an hour's lecture on his experiences as a Prisoner of War in Germany for 2 yrs. 3 months in the afternoon 3 to 4.

Nov. 14   Attendance is satisfactory. Armistice carnival and late celebrations made but little difference. Chn: came at 1.15 and left at 3.20 to enable them to get home and dress etc. for procession. The Staff made every effort to impress the full meaning of the anniversary home.

The celebrations mentioned above were the beginnings of East Hoathly's Carnival Society. A press report is headed "Victory Ball. Enjoyable Night at East Hoathly" and reports that the village was decorated with flags and "The Boys" who had been demobilised were happy to feel they were at home and so "a little bonfire was lit in the square". An impromptu ball took place in the King's Head Clubroom and most people wore fancy dress. The children were allowed to join in and a little cart decorated with flags and fairy lights was pulled by them and two clowns, and the whole procession visited all the principal houses in the village where speeches were made. The dancing and music continued into the early hours of the morning.

Mr Alec Jones with Class 2 in 1924

From about the 1920's the entries in the Log Books are more concerned with visits of speech therapists, Education Welfare Officers and the County Psychologist; with visits from officials inspecting the children, their teeth and their hair and officials inspecting buildings, furniture, playground, water supply, dinners and milk. The following excerpts are just a small selection of the more interesting entries.

1920

July 26   The Headmaster with permission of the L.E.A. will be absent for a fortnight attending the special course of Lectures for Schoolmasters as invited by the East Sussex Agric. Comtt.

This special course was held at the South Eastern Agricultural College, Wye and was entitled the Life History of the Apple Tree and dealt with its botanical, chemical, entomological and cultural aspects by means of lectures, laboratory work and demonstrations in the plantations.

May 29   …Report of H.M.I. (E. F. Davidson, Esq.) "This school continues to do good work; both Managers and teachers are to be complimented on the results of their efforts and their interest in it. The Head Master is keen and enthusiastic and it is to his leadership and control that much of the success is due. A quiet and orderly air of industry pervades all the classes and there is ample evidence that the scholars strive to do their best. A very satisfactory standard of efficiency is reached and the children are learning to be independent and resourceful. There are at present no practical classes in Housewifery or Cookery for girls nor in Handicraft for senior boys. The gardens are in excellent order but the boys in the class for the second or third years are repeating the first year's course. The Infants are kindly managed but as too much dependence is placed on class methods of instruction they are not kept fully occupied and they are not so well able to help themselves as they might be."…

The Managers replied to this report stating that the old classroom was available for cookery classes provided a suitable range could be fixed in place of the ordinary grate now existing, and the new building erected by the Managers last year could be used for woodwork if sufficient tools could be provided. It was well lit, but without a fireplace. Mr. Edwin Young replied that the sub-committee could not see their way to sanctioning the expenditure for the necessary equipment. The Master began a woodworking class with the permission of the Managers, provided expenditure was kept as low as possible.

Cookery classes for the girls commenced in 1926 when the girls travelled to Laughton, but a new Cookery and Craft centre was set up in Uckfield in 1928 - an easier journey for the East Hoathly pupils and the facilities were better. Later still a centre was established at Ringmer, the East Hoathly children attending this until 1953, then reorganisation took place as part of the Butler Education Act and the secondary modern school was opened at Ringmer for children of eleven plus. This school was well equipped for domestic science, woodwork and rural science as well as the ordinary classrooms.

July 12   School Cricket VI visit Maresfield to meet Fletching to play for 1st place in Div. iii. East Hoathly won on 1st Innings by 36 runs and win Divn. Shield.

July 28   Headmaster absent (afternoon) to attend the presenting of Trophies to the successful Cricket XIs in the Final and Divisional contests. East Hoathly receiving shield for Div. iii.

Taking part in these organized games was causing problems in the school's finances and the Correspondent wrote to Edwin Young asking for a grant. In November 1923 the Gardening Class had made a net profit of £2 10s. 7d. and they decided that this should be divided between the boys and girls to meet some of the expenses incurred in travelling to the Cricket and Stoolball matches.

1925

Dec. 23   Children given girls cloaks boys jerseys by Lt. Col. L. C. F. Thompson for many years a Manager and who has given every scholar the above gift at Christmas since 1911. The above gentleman passed away Dec. 7th just a few days after ordering the above.

1928

Nov. 13   Death of pupil R. Wickson at school on Thurs. last took place in Princess Alice Hospital from result of a fall aged 8.

1929

Jan. 15   Eighteen girls and 13 boys are to attend Uckfield Practical Centre today. The Girls for both morng. and aftern. and 6 boys in the morning and 7 in the afternoon. They are to be conveyed from E. H. and back by local carrier (E. R. Burchett) under agreement with L.E.A.

June 13   Royal County (Sussex) Show held at B'tn. Competition (Elem. Schools) of a forest tree in colour or pencil. Frank Turner awarded "Second Prize" for Oak-tree and studies on same.

Dec. 5   Another terrible gale of wind and rain only 63 present several had to be dried. It should be recorded that the majority of scholars now on books live a very long way from the school and hence the poor attendance on really boisterous days.

1930

May 7   Dr. Dunstan visited …Also colours of hairs and eyes of all children were examined and recorded.

1931

July 9   This morning the eldest children went to survey district N. and W. of Halland, being absent from quarter to ten till 12 o'clock…

July 23   The eldest children again took their hectographed sheets to complete the classes of fields around East Hoathly. This work is now finished and I am sending the Ordnance Sheet back to Lewes today.

1932

July 5   Fred Burtenshaw has been awarded 2nd prize in the chns. competition for a sketch in colour. Mrs. Campbell Johnstone came in this morning and handed him the prize - 12s. 6d.

July 25   Two girls - Joan Griffen and Diane Garlick - have passed the entrance examination to the Secondary Girls School at Lewes - they commence there in September.

1933

Nov. 21   Marks and little drawings have been seen on the desks (new ones) and the children have been punished with writing lines for this act…

1935

May 27   While playing cricket in the field during the dinner hour, Fred Eade was struck in the face by the ball and received a cut forehead. I sent him to the Nursing Home where the wound was dressed, after which he returned to school. Nurse advised him to consult Dr. Orchard this evening…

May 28   Fred Eade present again today. Told by doctor that the cut would be better left untouched.

May 29   Filled in insurance form relating to accident and forwarded to Lewes.

June 19   School closed this afternoon as we were competing in the Uckfield & District School Sports at Uckfield…Robert Hoad aged 10 won the Junior Long Jump….

1936

May 11   In payment of 10s. the East Hoathly Cricket Club granted permission for the boys to use the Cricket Field for Wednesday games and practice on two evenings a week, also for the girls to play their Stoolball games there each Wednesday.

June 9   I took a party of 33 children to the Aldershot Tattoo to-day…

1937

Apr. 14   …Although the fires are usually unlit at this time of the year, the weather has been so cold that most days we have had to light the fires.

Apr. 15   Miss Wenham, who taught in this school for over forty years was buried at East Hoathly today. The children subscribed towards a wreath and Miss Colebrook obtained leave of absence (half an hour) to attend the funeral.

Dec. 1   P. P. applied for admission to this school today. He stated that he formerly attended Rushlake Green School, and had now moved to Chiddingly. I discovered that he had been living in Chiddingly for more than a year…After school I went to Chiddingly and saw Mr. Sturdy, who informed me that P. P. was a pupil at his school, having attended as recently as yesterday. He had been sent to wash as he was so dirty, and evidently, this decided him to apply for admission to this school.

1939

Feb. 24   I was absent this afternoon attending a sale of poultry appliances…

Mar. 16   Mr. O. R. Stevenson, Poultry Adviser gave a talk on "poultry" to Class 1 from 3.25 to 4 o'clock today.

Mar. 28   At 11 a.m. today I went to Mountfield, Horam to collect the 150 sitting eggs for the school…

1940

Mar. 4   There was no school this morning as the supply of coke was exhausted. In the afternoon school was held in the Chapel.

Jun 26   …No milk has been received this week, Mr. Cottingham having discontinued the supply owing to shortage of petrol.

1941

Apr. 22   …Whole timetable given over to practising either in school or village hall, for War Weapons Week concert…

Apr. 28   £20 17s. 6d. realised for Concert. This banked in P.O. as loan to Government for duration of war.

1944

Feb. 9   10 a.m. Gas mask inspection by air raid wardens. 2.30 p.m. M. of I. film at Village Hall. All children attended by permission of Education Authorities.

1947

Sept. 12   The senior children attended a W.I. meeting this afternoon to hear Mr. Seth-Smith, the "Zoo Man" talk on "My Animal Friends".

1951

Oct. 24   I accompany 20 senior children on visit to Dicker Potteries this afternoon.

1954

June 25   The "Top Juniors" 27 had a days outing to the London Zoo, accompanied by the Headmaster, Mr. Dobbs, Mrs. Harris and Mrs. Costick. The party left by coach at 9 p.m. arriving Zoo at 12.0 and returned to East Hoathly at 8.30 p.m. Despite adverse weather conditions, the day was much enjoyed.

1955

July 11   The school was closed today for an outing to Portsmouth. Twenty seven children in the top class, two members of staff and two parents participated. Leaving at 9.00 a.m. the party toured the "Victory" and was taken on a boat trip round Portsmouth Harbour. The coach arrived back at 8.30 p.m.

1961

July 7   Friday. School closed for annual outing of Upper Juniors. This took the form of a coach trip to London lunch in Hyde Park, visits to the science and Natural History Museums and tea at Streatham…

1962

Jan. 11   …A gale ripped tiles from the N.E. edge of the roof of the Infants building, then caused bricks in that gable to collapse at 10.55 a.m. Many of these fell just outside the Infants W.C.'s but fortunately, because of the weather all children were in school…

July 16   …A number of children were late this morning having been to see the Queen en route from Uckfield to Lewes. Mrs. Jackson was at the Lewes reception for the Queen ex officio as an official of Lewes Ladies Guild…

July 27   …Mrs. M. C. Jackson left today. On Monday she is attending a course in Arts and Crafts at Loughborough for a fortnight and in September is taking a post near Winchester. She was presented with a set of table mats and a book token.

1963

Jan. 21   The pipes frozen at the mains. Plumbers free one but not the others so water has to be carried…No relief in the cold weather attendance below 80% and the school fires need careful watching to keep a reasonable temperature. Still carrying water to kitchen and washbasins.

Feb. 1   …Mains water pipe burst because the meter had frozen…Burst discovered by headmaster under floor boards in Infants annexe…

Feb. 6   …Incipient blizzard. It seems probable that the bus children should be sent home as a precautionary measure but snow stopped at 11 a.m…

March 25   ….Two boys and two girls admitted. One of the girls…went home at 9.15 (without permission) because "none of the children had spoken to her". Her brother went home to see if she was safely there and both returned at 10.40 a.m. There was no further trouble.

1967

Jan. 5   School reopened today. 52 children on roll.

Jan. 9   Mr. Howells visited today to discuss the fall in numbers at the school. He is to try to find out details of proposed building programmes in the village.

March. 13 A team of four (Duncan Gaylor, Pauline Sibbett, John Copper and Susan Pelling) won the silver cup in the Inter-school quiz. Each child was presented with a book token value £1 1s.

1971

Oct. 22   100 years of State Education. The school was open this evening. We had organised a display of work of present day and samples of work of former times. The old log books, admission registers, etc. were of great interest and the numerous photographs of earlier days were most interesting…

1973

Oct. 11   …Class 1 went to the Village Hall at 3 p.m. to hear Mr. Blackmore give a talk on his experiences with the Sioux on a Reservation in N. America. He gave an interesting historical review of Indian life and customs. The children particularly enjoyed his rendering of Red Indian songs and sign language and were most impressed by the Indian costume which he wore.

Nov. 15   …The Government has announced that under their Emergency Powers, schools which are heated by electricity had to turn their heaters off…

Nov. 16   The Government has decided to allow schools to use electricity, but to save current where possible.

1974

Jan. 3   A part of 93 visited the Devonshire Theatre to see "Jack and the Beanstalk"…

May 14   This morning Mr. Stamp, Health Officer, came to inspect our pool and to our horror all the water had drained away…it was obvious that there were four slashes in the bottom lining, which loked as if they had been done deliberately…Police continue investigating but have not found the culprits.

1977

Feb. 28   ….During the holiday a great deal of thick clay and mud was thrown all over the school walls and windows. This was reported to the police and Mr. Farmer found the culprits, only one of whom lives in the village. He was made to come to the school and house and clean up as much mess as possible…

1978

May 10   The whole school went on a trip on the Paddle Steamer Waverley. A most enjoyable outing marred by bad behaviour of older children from various Comprehensive Schools.

Nov. 1   It is with great regret that we have to record the sudden death of the headmistress, Mrs. K. D. Mosley. Mrs. Mosley had been unwell the previous day…School will function as usual.

1979

Oct. 1   Children brought in sunflowers grown in sponsorship in aid of Sussex Nature Conservation and School Funds. The tallest was 3m. 20cm. grown by Emma Farmer. In the afternoon a photographer from the Courier newspaper came and took a picture of Emma and her plant.

1980

Feb. 25 ... Three tradesmen called - one to fit a new staff notice board, another to repair the staffroom fire and a third to replace all the classroom bulb holders...

June 27 A remarkable day for weather. Among

several heavy showers was one tremendous downpour of hailstones which covered the playground to a depth of 3 or 4 centimetres ... Surprisingly the shower was not noticed at either Whitesmith or Halland.

July 11 ...School outing to London and the Royal Tournament.

School Cricket Team 1922. Back row, left to right: Alec Jones; George Barden; William Shanks; Charlie Walters; Albert Heasman; Albert Hall. Front row, left to right: Alex Stewart; Charlie Bishop; Sydney Lawrence; Jack Topping; Donald Stewart.

The Garden Class had been started in 1912 at the wish of H.M.I., Mr. Garland and the necessary tools were purchased locally and the seeds from Sutton & Son. The tools had cost £2 17s. 9d. and the seeds 18s. 1d. Garden trugs were also bought from A. F. Rich, a local firm, to the value of 7s. In November 1912 a Mr. W. Goaring visited the school to inspect the proposed plots for the school gardens. In July 1913 the aptly named H.M.I., Mr. C. Boutflower, visited the gardens and commented that a good start had been made on them. He said it was satisfactory that "an additional 5 rods would be available another season which will bring the total area up to 20 rods and will enable the scope of the teaching to be broadened so as to include something beyond the cultivation of vegetables only".

In December 1913 the gardening class also cost a further £2 9s. 3d. made up as follows:- Manure 14s. 0d. Soot and lime 2s. 0d. Pea and bean sticks 4s. 3d. and rent of the plot 8s. 4d. The seed requisition had asked for one quart peas Prince of Wales 1s. 6d., which the committee felt was unnecessary as there were two other varieties mentioned. They also refused permission for a further 4 draw hoes as the full complement had been supplied at the commencement of the class. The cost of flower seeds was reduced from 5s. to 1s. and the request for one dozen currant and gooseberry bushes was deferred until Mr. Goaring had considered the scheme for fruit culture generally.

In 1916 a further order was placed - Pea and bean sticks 5s. 0d. Manure 14s. 0d. Seeds 14s. 9d. Rent of garden 8s. 4d. The ground had been judged as "very poor" at the last inspection and in need of a "more liberal allowance of manure." The seeds were obtained from Elphicks of Lewes.

In 1922 the expenditure had risen to - Seeds £1 10s. 8d., Pea and Bean Sticks 5s. Rent 15s.

In June 1914 Mr. Goaring again inspected the school gardens and the Managers were sent a letter from the Education Committee, presumably in response to Mr. Goaring's inspection, asking why no permission had been sought for the conversion of an outhouse into a tool shed, the conversion costing £1 7s. 6d. Their reply was that the doorless brick building already existed and in order to keep the tools safe the work was put in hand immediately. The council agreed to pay for the work done.

The Gardening Class photographed sometime in the 1920s. From left to right: Jim Branley; Bruce Allcorn; William Novis; Will Sommerset; Thomas Burtenshaw; Ron Allcorn (at back); Alf Roberts; Dennis Staplehurst; Thomas Crowhurst; Bernard Ballard; James Woodhams; Will Laker.

SCHOOL, CHURCH, & RECTORY, EAST HOATHLY. 5013.

A postcard showing the school gardens. The school buildings are on the left with two haystacks in front; the church is in the middle and the old Rectory is to the right. There is a row of cabbages in the foreground.

On the 5th July 1916 the entry reads: - Chn: provided over 50 cabbages for Sailors this fortnight.

In October 1921 the School Gardening Class won the Challenge Spade presented by Mr. W. Troy for the best Garden. The gardens had been exceptionally well managed and the Education Committee conveyed hearty congratulations to the Managers, Teachers and Scholars. The School was granted a half holiday on the strength of this success. The silver spade arrived on the 25th November and was fixed on the school wall.

In 1922 the Silver Spade was won by Newhaven, but East Hoathly's garden received a special mention in the Horticultural Expert's Report. The Challenge Spade was again awarded to East Hoathly in 1927.

In 1913 the produce from the garden was sold and the amount of £3 5s. 11d. was raised. Regrettably in July 1914 K. F. was punished by the Headmaster for stealing the money! The highest amount was £4 15s. 9d. realised in 1924.

In November 1923 the Gardening Class had made a net profit of £2 10s. 7d. and they decided that this should be divided between the boys and girls to meet some of the expenses incurred in travelling to the Cricket and Stoolball matches.

In 1921 the school entered the Flower Show of the Women's Institute

and won 1st prize for the Best Collection of Six Vegetables.

In June 1928 H.M.I. Mr. E. F. Davidson reported the following:- "Gardening forms an important feature in the teaching of this rural school and is correlated with several other branches of the ordinary instruction. There is evidence of earnest work on the plots, the boys also make useful notes of the Headmaster's lessons in School and their drawings are above the average in merit. It is important that the plots should be cropped each year in accordance with a previously arranged plan entered in each boy's note book and careful accounts of income and expenditure in connection with their garden should also be kept by the boys. No fruit is grown in the School Garden but the Headmaster obtains permission to take the class for occasional lessons to a neighbouring orchard a privilege which is much appreciated and of which full advantage is taken. He is also interested in Poultry keeping and as at present only 29 per cent of the Senior Children eligible by age are receiving practical instruction it is suggested that a course in Poultry keeping should be started here…"

In 1932 15 boys were taking the Gardening Classes and those not involved were in school drawing. It was recommended by the Inspector in 1936 that more flowers should be grown and in 1946 the children were being instructed by a film on gardening shown in the Village Hall. There is no mention of the Gardening Classes after about 1960.

CENTENARY CELEBRATIONS
1965

The School and village have lived through many momentous national events, but from the log books it would seem that they touched daily life of the School very little. Coronations, Royal weddings and such like resulted in a day's holiday, the advent of the first World War merits a mention in brackets, a Roll of Honour and a talk by an ex-P.O.W., but very little else. The events of the second World War are conspicuous by their absence - at the outset of the hostilities it is recorded that the Managers considered trenches should be dug in Church Field for the protection of the children. Part of the same field was to be used for a garden for the evacuees. Unfortunately by November because of the rain the trenches had silted up and permission was given for the Head Master to have them filled in and to use them as a garden for the duration of the war.

The evacuees numbered 205, and brought the numbers of children on the school register to 102 but it was found possible to provide them all with full time education by using the school, the Wesleyan Chapel and the vestry. On 24th June 1940 the Chaucer children were evacuated to Wales and school work progressed normally. There was some shortage of fuel for the fires and on occasions no milk deliveries because of lack of petrol. Gas masks were provided and subjected to regular inspections by the A.R.P. Wardens. I am sure that there were many disruptions to school work because of air raids, etc., but unfortunately the log books at this time are more concerned with the teachers and their comings and goings.

There is one further event which cannot be left out of such a book as this and that is the Centenary celebrations in 1965 and I give below several extracts from the log book:

Jan. 19 Tues. On this day the school celebrated the centenary of its Dedication (Opening) Service. At 9.45 a.m. a service was held in the Parish Church. The Lord Bishop of Lewes preached the sermon, the Rector, Rev. F. L. Taylor, conducted the service; the headmaster C. C. Harry, B.A. read the lesson. The church was very nearly full. A retiring collection (in aid of Church Repair Fund) realised £18 13s. 2d. Among those present were the Deputy Education Officer, J. R. Jones, Esq., M.A., Mrs. E. S. Harry, Mr. G. Fleet, M.A. (County Inspectors of Schools), Managers and past Managers, members of the Parish Council (of which the headmaster is Chairman), Mr. Fred Jones, son of Mr. Alec Jones, Head master from 1896-1930, and Mrs. Jones, wives of managers and councillors, Lady Hunting. After the service, flowers were placed on the graves of Capt. Clements (founder and benefactor), Rev. Langdale (founder and benefactor), Rev. Harbord (benefactor), Mr. F. Jones (Headmaster 1871-1891), Mr. T. Jones (Headmaster 1891-6), Mr. A. Jones (Headmaster 1896-1930). The Lord Bishop spent some time in the school with the children.

At 2 p.m. five octogenarians, Mrs. Cornwell, Mrs. Finch, Mrs. Hall, Mr. Guy and Mr. A. Starnes, all educated at the school answered childrens questions about life and education in the village during the 90s. The Rector presided.

In the evening from 6 p.m. the school was open to visitors. There was a display of childrens' work, text books and teaching aids. At 7.30 p.m. after a short P. Teacher Assn. business meeting, Mrs. E. S. Harry (County Inspector) gave a talk on the history of the school as recorded in the log books. The interest of the audience (about 90-100) which completely filled the larger Infant room was apparent by the fact that in the one and a quarter hours it lasted, there was complete absence of coughing, shuffling or indeed of any movement. The last visitor left at 10 p.m. Officials present at this meeting were Mr. G. Fleet, M.A., Miss I. M. Johnson, B.A. and S. Hurst, County Inspectors.

A display of school groups dating from 1883, the log books, old time tables etc. in the school office attracted very considerable attention.

The weather throughout the day was ideal.

The headmaster must record the great help he received from his teaching staff, Mrs. E. L. Cottingham and Mrs. M. G. Barden; the cook, Miss E. Hook (for catering both morning and evening), Mrs. Berry, the clerical assistant, and Mr. W. G. Heasman, the caretaker. The officers of the Parent-Teacher Association were also most helpful. The production of the "Order of Service" …was organised by Mrs. E. S. Harry at the cost of £1 10s. for 300 copies.

Jan 20 Wed.   Today we realise how very fortunate we were with our weather yesterday. From early morning a damp snow has been driven almost horizontally by a bitter wind. The surfaces of all secondary roads have been made most treacherous. In all my time here I have never seen the floor in the Junior porch so wet. Despite this only seven children are absent, and none late. Many top coats are so wet that I (and the staff) have to dry them on the fire guards and chairs near the stoves. The work displayed on the cupboards etc. has been taken down, the display of photographs, log books, etc. including handwriting (ink) by Mrs. Finch in 1898 (age 6) and hemming of handkerchief which she did when 4 years old stored away or returned so that we are back to normal and school lessons are resumed…

21st Jan. Thurs. Work as usual but the children are excited and not settling down well. The appearance of their arithmetic suffers. Following a homily by the headmaster there is a distinct improvement and the written work in Geography this afternoon is at least as well done as usual…The snow is 'lying' frozen.

Jan. 22   There being a moderate thaw, the playground has been a filthy mess. Despite the fact that large areas were brushed clear, several children managed to fall and make their clothes wet. T. and R. F. were 'dried off' in front of the stove, but N. I. was so wet that he had to sit in his duffle coat while his pullover, shirt and knickers were dried on the stove. So ends an eventful week in the history of the school.

Jan. 24 Sun.   Sir Winston L. Spencer Churchill died this morning at the age of 90. He was the greatest figure of his age and especially to be noted for preserving freedom as a result of the 1939-45 war.

Jan. 25 Mon. The shouting and the tumult having died we are fully back to normal…Following the easy and free atmosphere of last week the children in all classes needed some settling down.

Jan. 26   …The headmaster went to the village to discuss with the newsagent an order for photographs of the Nativity Play, the school and the Bishop of Lewes, Rev. Morrell, with the children…During morning break the headmaster and older boys returned to the village hall cups etc. borrowed for the Centenary celebrations. The results of the Tables Test today were 'ragged'.

and so on to the latest celebrations - the opening of the newly extended and refurbished school in March 1992. East Hoathly school buildings have been greatly enlarged, altered and rearranged over the years, but I am sure that Captain Clements, the Reverend Langdale and Squire Gilliatt and all the Jones family would thoroughly approve and be justly proud of the pupils and their teachers, and the newest and brightest alterations.

Pupils, teachers and helpers – Summer of 1996

Extra space created in the roof area of the school

The Junior School choir photographed in East Hoathly Church at the School Nativity Play, 1996

The school opened in 1865 with quite a few items of equipment missing. We are told of the arrival of the master's desk and the governess' table over a week after opening day, and the easel and blackboard and some books arrive in March. A new blind was ordered for the Class Room and an eight day clock was presented in April by William Gilliatt, the local squire.

There was no lighting at all. The timetable was altered in the winter to accommodate the darker afternoons and to enable the children to get home before darkness set in. However in November 1871 it is mentioned that the Reverend Borrodaile had promised two new lamps for Night School.

Heating was by coal or coke fires, which were not lit until the middle of November. There would appear to have been nowhere to dry the children's outer clothing when they were caught in the rain on their way to school, so they were sent home again. It would also seem from some entries that it was not possible to dry the children's wet clothing at home either and as they had no spare garments they were on occasions unable to attend school the following day. Children were kept at school and dried in the School House for the first time on October 1901 and it is not until June 1903 that fires are specially lit in order to dry the wet children, and presumably this is done as it is now the County Council's responsibility for the cost of heating.

The classroom was supplied with a thermometer, so some check was kept on the temperature. An enquiry on the 21st March 1912 elicits the information that the two fireplaces in the infant schoolroom are protected with fire guards which require a little repair, and the four fireplaces in the mixed room are without proper guards. The Managers recommended that all fireplaces in the mixed room should have proper guards fitted.

In 1936 after an inspection which revealed that the heating in the school was not up to standard, it was decided to upgrade with Tortoise stoves, but there is no record of this work being carried out. However there was a Tortoise stove in the main room in 1941 as this required repairs and the Managers resolved to install one in the main Infant School during the summer vacation of 1943.

In 1962 there were still fires to be lit but by 1973 the school had night storage heaters.

There was no caretaker; it would seem that possibly the master and pupil teachers cleaned the premises together with some of the older pupils - certainly Mr. Frederick Jones and the pupil teachers cleaned the school on his return in 1880.

When a caretaker was appointed he or she apparently worked with very little labour saving equipment as on November 6th 1973 the following entry reads: "...Mr. Tomlinson has agreed in principle that the school should be provided with a carpet sweeper or vacuum cleaner and some form of mechanical scrubber for the Marley tiled floors. He has promised to visit the school soon to see the position for himself and to assess the need for additional equipment…"

In the early days there were no school meals, and the children either went home to dinner, or if their journey was long, brought their meals with them in baskets.

Sports equipment was non-existent, the Reverend Langdale obtaining a football for the boys in December of the first year and giving them a lesson in their dinner hour. In 1871 the Reverend Borrodaile gave the boys another new football and it is recorded in August of that year that school is dismissed early at 3.30 so that the elder girls might go to Miss Borrodailes' house to take part in a game of stoolball. In 1891 Captain Clements gave the boys another football, and the Reverend Harbord, the "sporty" Rector, also provided a field rent free for their use.

In 1894 the head master bought two cricket bats and two stoolball bats from subscriptions given by friends of the parish. Games are now being played regularly with neighbouring parishes, and there is a Recreation Club.

Mr. J. G. Morgan, on taking up headship in 1935, found a shortage of sports equipment and began a subscriptions list to obtain funds, collecting £11 10s.

The children did play organized games during the school day, but at what date this came into being is not known. In February 1884 it is noted that recreation break at 10.30 "has a great influence on the health of the school in continued wet weather when the children are unable to obtain fresh air the classes seem to suffer from lassitude and that brightness is absent, which is indicative of mental activity." However, it is recorded on 2nd October 1912 that during the winter months there would be cardboard modelling and paper flower making or doll dressing instead of games.

In 1894 Mrs. Maples gave some games for the amusement of the pupils in the wet dinner hours, and in 1895 the Recreation Club provided some more. On October 16th 1901 the Reverend Harbord provided new games, and over the years many more gifts of dolls and games, and on one occasion a rocking horse, are given, mostly by the gentry of the village.

The children were taught music and in 1891 a concert was held, the proceeds of which were to be used to purchase a harmonium for the infant school, which would release the original harmonium, being repaired in Brighton, for use for Musical Drill.

Mr. Frederick Thomas Jones was very keen on drawing, and also in 1891 a blackboard for scale drawing was bought. In July 1892 his order of models and vases for Model Drawing arrived plus six "Object Lesson Specimens". There was also a system of drawing called "Free Arm" for which special boards were needed, and the children were photographed at their Free-arm lesson.

Mr. Alex Jones was just as keen on singing and was choir master, taking the choir to various festivals in London and Uckfield.

The subject of desks is not mentioned in the Log Books until the end of December 1891, when there would seem to be a shortage. This is brought up at the next Managers' meeting and Mr. Jones is told in March that two new desks are on order. They were Victor Dual desks which were received in April and after some thought were used in the Infant School and three new Reversible desks were to be ordered for the Mixed School. However, accommodation would seem to be somewhat short as these two dual desks were transferred from the Infants into the Classroom in May. On March 20th 1899 ten new Hallamshire desks, each seven feet long, were put into the main room. These apparently ended their lives as part of the school house garden shed. How many children can you fit onto a 7' desk in comfort?

In 1901 the infants' old desks were converted into suitable lengths for the small classroom as they were of much more use than the original ones bought in 1865. When the Gallery was removed, the Managers requested tables and chairs for the children, but the Authority sent them Dual desks instead.

In 1925 the Managers asked Mr. J. H. Baines, Director of Education for 18 infant dual tables and extra number of K.G. Chairs, as in the upper infant room they had to seat 40 or more children who were at that moment using 12 long desks of 4 seating. The Managers of East Hoathly School certainly knew what they wanted, but it is not recorded whether they were successful.

36 new dual desks arrived in February 1928. (The dual desks were iron bound with fixed seats.)

The school was given several pictures, the Rev. G. S. Wilson presenting a set of coloured plates illustrating grasses in 1895; Col. L. C. F. Thompson presented the school with a copy of Nelson's Last Signal and a copy of the Charge of the Light Brigade, both in oak frames; in 1901 he presented the School with "3 beautiful pictures of our Late Gracious Queen, of King Edward VII and of Queen Alexandria". and in 1914 he gave pictures of George V and Queen Mary, a hunting subject and a picture of the Boy Hero, Jack Cornwell. They were also presented with many interesting and unusual items for the School museum, which I hope was the success Mr. Jones envisaged. However, as my enquiries have only elicited memories of the ostrich egg, perhaps it did not have the impact he had hoped!

The first medical inspection was on 4th December 1908, it took three days and was presumably a great hit with the mothers as they took the opportunity of consulting the medical inspector personally. I rather fear the first visit by the dentist was not met with much enthusiasm by the children. His first recorded visit was 7th October 1921 and resulted in the treatment of 27 children. The following year he extracted teeth from 26 children, who were sent home, but they received their mark for the day. July 1st 1941 is the first mention of diphtheria immunisation.

In 1928 a singer sewing machine was supplied and on 29th February 1944, a gramophone; on January 15th 1946 a Smallwood upright piano was purchased with money raised at School concerts. On July 5th 1965 a Sobell Television set arrived for upper juniors. It was switched on for the first time on 8th July when at 11.30 a.m.

the Third Test Match between England and New Zealand was being shown, and the first over was watched, and at 2 p.m. the same afternoon the whole of Spotlight was seen - this programme dealing with the problems facing the Jews' plan for irrigating the Niger Desert.

On 31st May 1946 the Managers visited the school premises with a view to possibly bringing electricity into the school building from the canteen meter for use of a projector and wireless set. It was installed on 16th November 1946 into Junior and Senior classrooms and on 10th July 1947 curtains were fitted so the projector could be used in the junior room. The School house had been connected to the electricity supply by the Weald Electricity Supply Co. in 1934/5 when it cost £6 14s. 6d. or £5 4s. if the Church was also connected.

A new electric stove for the canteen was installed in 1951, the canteen having been opened on 7th September, 1942, when 50 dinners were served.

On 29th April 1955 a refrigerator was delivered to the canteen and an urn supplied for drinking water. And on 13th June 1967 it is recorded that the kitchen was demolished and the new one opened on 9th October of the same year.

The original water supply was, of course, from a well. In October 1903 it was suggested that surface water entering the well in the Master's garden should be stopped by raising the brickwork a couple of courses. The well was then to be cleaned and the water tested. Unfortunately the analysis was as follows: "The report of Mr. Farr, who had made an analysis of the water taken from the well in the Master's garden, was read. Of which the following is an extract: "The figures for albuminoid ammonia and Nitric acid are excessive and indicate that the water is contaminated. It is also excessively hard. It must be condemned as unfit for drinking, and is too hard for general domestic use". After a thorough consideration of the matter on the proposal of Mr. Jones, seconded by Col. Thompson it was put to the meeting and carried unanimously "that a new well be dug in the N.E. corner of the piece of ground rented for the master's garden, and that it be connected by an iron pipe with the school house yard, and that the old well be filled up when satisfactory water has been found…"

On the 31st March 1905 the water in the new well was again to be analysed, but we are not told of the results and in June of that year the master reported the bad condition of his rain water tank, which was ordered to be cleaned out.

In the summer of 1940 the School House was connected to mains water by the generosity of A. G. Howard and others.

In 1942 estimates were obtained for electric wiring to the cookhouse and the laying on of water provision to sink.

In 1943 it was resolved that the rain water well be made usable for the canteen and general purposes by having a pump fitted. In 1944 the caretaker was given a further 2s. 6d. per school week to see that the school canteen was supplied with sufficient water by rotary pump in the School house. It was agreed that the boys should not be allowed to do this work.

On the 9th September 1952 the House well used by the school and canteen ran dry and Hailsham R.D.C. ordered 400 gallons of water to be delivered. On 24th October there was a cloudburst and on 11th November the water delivery was cancelled, so presumably the well filled up again.

At the beginning of Spring term 1954 the electric pump in School House supplying water to the canteen was disconnected, as the school was between head teachers and the house was empty. Two boys fetched buckets of water from a nearby house.

In January 1957 there was an inquiry into water supplies to the N. E. Parishes of Hailsham R.D.C. and on 3rd April samples of water were taken and there was once again contamination in the well water.

But it was not until Saturday, 6th July 1957 that it is recorded that because the well water was found to be badly contaminated, two 200 gallon tanks were placed beside the Infants building. They were filled when necessary by the Hailsham

R.D.C. with water from their reservoirs. The well in the School House garden was cleaned out but because of its closeness to the churchyard and to other possible sources of contamination, the Public Health Dept. thought it was dangerous as a source of drinking water.

On 5th December 1960 trenching was begun in order to lay pipes for mains water supply and this was completed during the Christmas holidays.

On 14th September 1956 a false ceiling was considered for conserving warmth in winter - this was removed in the latest building works finished in 1992.

Swimming lessons at Deanland Wood Caravan Park, Golden Cross commenced on 13th May 1964 and on 5th September 1972, the swimming pool on the school premises was built, finally being in use on 11th June the following year after three years hard work and many set backs.

Carrying on the tradition of maypole dancing at an open afternoon for parents and friends

Reception Class 1996. Nativity play.

PRESENTATIONS

Miss Benham. In the afternoon of the 30th August 1875 when school broke up for the summer holidays, Miss Benham, the Infant Mistress, "was presented with a testimonial of the value of £5 6s. 6d. by the Gentry and inhabitants of Easthothly." She was also given a gold watch, presented by Captain Clements on behalf of the villagers. She had been with the school for nearly nine years.

Captain and Mrs. Clements. On December 12th 1887 there is the following entry "…On Thursday afternoon the whole school was dismissed a little before time to welcome Captain Clements the Secretary on his return to the village after his wedding trip. The inhabitants drew his carriage through the village amid general rejoicing."

And in 1888 "…The teachers, and past and present scholars presented Captain Clements with an art volume, Ebor's Egypt. The presentation had been delayed owing to the time occupied in re-binding. Captain and Mrs. Clements have gained the affection and gratitude of the old and present children and teachers by the interest they have for so many years taken in their welfare."

Frederick Thomas Jones. In January 1888 Frederick Thomas Jones left the school for York Training College and the Managers, teachers, scholars and friends presented him with Macauley's History of England and a "beautiful box of instruments."

Frederick Thomas succeeded his father as Headmaster on the 25th March 1891. He had been an Assistant in the Higher Grade School, York Place, Brighton. He unfortunately died on the 29th April 1896 when his brother, Ernest Alexander, was appointed Head Teacher in his place.

Miss E. A. Jones. On the 3rd November 1905 Miss E. A. Jones who had been with the school for 22 months resigned, having accepted a post at her old school at Lampeter. The children and teachers presented her with a gold brooch and copy of Cowper's poems.

Miss E. M. Hunt. Miss Hunt taught at the school for 22 years. On the occasion of her marriage to Mr. T. Hoad she was presented with a brass fire-side companion and a brass mounted glass fire screen from the pupils; and a silver mounted oak salad bowl and servers inscribed "Presented to Miss E. M. Hunt by the staff of East Hoathly School, on the occasion of her marriage, 27/8/24."

Miss Rhoda Wenham. Miss Rhoda Wenham taught at the School from June 1887 until March 1929. She had served as Assistant Mistress under the headship of E. A. Jones, who said he had always "found her loyal dutiful and zealous in every respect." The School Managers each subscribed 10s. so that she could buy a book of her choice and they also presented her with a travelling case. She received an armchair from the staff and an eiderdown from the scholars. She died at Halland in 1937 aged 70.

Ernest Alexander Jones. Ernest Alexander Jones tendered his resignation in 1930 which was received by the Managers with the deepest regret. They wrote him an exceedingly complimentary letter. In April of that year there is the following entry:- "School closed for Easter to reopen on Thurs. 1st May owing to change of Head Teachers. At the close of school the Chairman of Managers officially wished Mr. E. A. Jones "Goodbye" as the headmaster and J. Campbell-Johnstone, Esq., J.P. on behalf of old and present scholars and Staff presented Mr. Jones with a China Cabinet and an oxidised fire side companion set in polished silver of Kerb, screen and a pair of fire-irons etc. … Mr. Jones thanked all and briefly replied."

On the 22nd July the Managers presented Mr. and Mrs. Jones with an inscribed silver fruitstand.

Mrs. Jones tendered her resignation to take effect on the 31st July. She had taught at the school for many years, (her first position) and the children and staff presented her with a period pewter tea pot, sugar basin, milk and hot water jugs together with a gold pendant and chain.

There were 22 applicants for the vacancy of head teacher and Miss Eliza Dyason Hazle was chosen. Her first requisition list caused several comments from the Managers on the number of articles required! Miss Hazle remained with the school until 1934.

Ernest Alexander Jones had succeeded his brother in 1896. He had opened Crowborough Board School. He married Alice Elizabeth Gifkins in 1898 and he died in April 1946

Colonel L. C. F. Thompson. Colonel L. C. F. Thompson of Hesmonds was a Manager of the School and he had originally given cloaks with hoods to the girls together with a brooch and capes and a pin to the boys as a Coronation gift. Two years later the boys were given a "cardigan, jacket or jersey" instead of capes and the girls received a long cloak with hood. They in turn presented him with a silver mounted and engraved hunting crop.

In 1916 the gifts changed to a long scarlet cloak for the girls (with hood) and a blue jersey for the boys. The cloaks in particular are remembered as being extremely warm and very durable. They were all wool, and all the children were individually measured, this undertaking necessitating a day off school work. The garments were specially ordered from a firm in Wales. Whilst most parents were happy their children should receive this generous gift, others thought of it as "charity".

The gifts continued each year until 1925 when Colonel Thompson died on the 7th December a few days after ordering the garments.

Miss Colebrook. Miss Colebrook had been an assistant teacher for 30 years and on 31st August 1938 she was presented with a silver rose bowl.

J. G. Morgan. Mr. Morgan was presented with a "suitably inscribed" silver cigarette case on his resignation in 1940. He took up new duties as Head Teacher of Westham Senior Council Mixed School.

Miss Thorns. Miss Thorns retired at the end of winter term in 1960 after eighteen years with the school and she was presented with a wrist watch.

"Today I finished reading the draft of *"As Clean a Lot of Children as He Had Ever Seen"* by Mrs. Seabrook. The years pass so quickly but the log books help us to recall the challenges and changes in the life of the village school.

It confirms my belief that education isn't only measured in terms of levels or grades, but in the quality of life and the people we meet.

Children, whatever generation, are still children, full of curiosity and fun, so some things go on in much the same way as before. I wonder if the present entries will make such fascinating reading in future years. Time will tell."

Mrs. P. Duff, MA., Headteacher.

William Batchelor Kingswood	January 1865 - August 1871
Frederick Jones	August 1871 - April 1879
Hugh Gould Webb	April 1879 - October 1880
Frederick Jones	November 1880 - 1891
Frederick Thomas Jones	March 1891 - April 1896
James Wilkins	May 1896 - May 1896
R. White	June 1896 - July 1896 (Temporary)
Ernest Alexander Jones	August 1896 - April 1930
Miss Eliza Dyason Hazle	May 1930 - October 1934
J. G. Morgan	October 1934 - September 1940
Mrs. Ivy H. Burgess	September 1940 - December 1945
Mrs. Phyllis Bright	March 1946 - December 1953
Miss J. M. Sinden	January 1954 (Temporary)
C. C. Harry, B.A.	February 1954 - July 1965
Mrs. K. D. Mosley	September 1965 - November 1978
J. D. Fry	February 1979 - December 1982
Elizabeth O'Donnell	January 1983 - April 1983 (Acting Head)
Mrs. Marianne Randall	April 1983 - 1988
Mrs. Jackie Morris	1988 - 1993
Mrs. Paula Duff	1993 -

A VISION STATEMENT

Experience an excellent education for all
All curriculum areas well taught
Supportive, sympathetic sharing of ideas
Teamwork at its best.

High standards, clear goals
Openness, open-hearted, open-minded, open doors
An association which draws all people together
Traditions, school and leisure time shared
Home and school in partnership
Links in school with home and the whole community
You are always welcome.

Children come first
Enjoyment and respect for the environment
Pride in our achievements.

Our vision is for East Hoathly School to be a school where parents and children can trust in the professionalism of the Governors and staff. To be a team of people from the cleaning staff to the Chair of Governors, a group of people who always care and contribute in a positive manner to the different aspects of the school. A group of people who provide a balanced education for the children. developing their personal, social, physical, spiritual and intellectual abilities to each child's highest level.

The concern of the school is to provide effective education for each child. To help children gain independence and confidence in their own achievements. All staff are sympathetic to children's individual differences, their varying needs and strengths. The experiences, activities provided for the children, are planned to reflect the children's different stages of development and interest. The school is a place where parents are involved in/participate in, the development of their children working together with the teachers over agreed aims of education.

Everyone at East Hoathly puts children first in order to help them succeed in life. Parents and staff all play a vital part in the children's education. We believe that the very best way to achieve our vision is to provide the children with a carefully structured learning environment which provides opportunites for a broad and balanced curriculum ensuring continuity and progression. Children learn best through 'doing', ideally all activities are derived from the child's own experience first. We see it as our responsibility to provide our children with a rich, exciting and variable learning environment. To stimulate their curiosity, encouraging experiential learning developed and lead through appropriately timed acts of intervention.

The aim of our School Management Plan is to enhance the quality of teaching and learning but at the centre of this must be the child. Our School Management Plan sets out how we aim to achieve these principles over a period of time.

OUR CHILDREN ARE THE FUTURE

East Hoathly School aims to provide a secure and happy environment which encourages attitudes and qualities which can lead to high levels of achievement and sometimes "excellence". A school where children and adults work together to create a sense of purpose and an understanding of the world around us.

Povoß.HT. 1994.

Yesterday is already a dream and tomorrow is only a vision. But today, well lived, makes every yesterday a dream of happiness and every tomorrow a vision of hope.

(Sanskrit)